ADVANCE PRAISE FOR

*The Art and Craft of*

# STORYTELLING

Nancy Lamb is at her usual high standard. Of the more than two hundred books about writing on my shelves, this is the best single reference I have. Read this book. Use it. Your writing will be better for it.

>—Charles Connor, Founding Director, The Harriette
>Austin Writing Program, The University of Georgia

I've written for television for many years, functioning like the piano player who can play anything but can't read music. Nancy Lamb's book taught me how read the music of writing. If you want to write, read this book. If you already write but want to read the music, read this book—and keep it handy.

>—Joe Halderman, Producer/Writer, CBS News
>and 48 HOURS MYSTERY

The essential guidebook for anyone who wants to write a book. Comprehensive and clear, it is a must read for new authors embarking on their writing journey.

>—Peter Guber, Chairman and CEO,
>Mandalay Entertainment Group

Nancy Lamb's experience and instruction informs, excites, and shows me how to do it! She's on my side, rooting for me, investing all that she's learned in writing her books so can I tackle my own projects. She knows the storytelling process inside and out, and she makes teaching it not only a story in itself, but a story you want to live.

>—Sheila Bender, author and publisher of
>WritingItReal.com

From her comprehensive breakdown of genres to her eight approaches to story structure to her process for creating unforgettable characters, Nancy Lamb's book overflows with incredibly useful advice, tips, and techniques. Her tone is inspirational, gently encouraging, and filled with warm good-humor—reading it is like being led to the secret well of creativity by your best friend.

—Eric Elfman, author, screenwriter, writing coach

*The Art and Craft of Storytelling* is articulate, cohesive, insightful, and comprehensive. It takes every question I've been asked by a student or have discussed with fellow writers and answers it—not just summarily, but in depth and with valuable examples. A writing book of this caliber is a rare find, and I recommend it for all aspiring writers, as well as established writers looking for an excellent refresher course.

—Dale Griffiths Stamos, playwright
and SBWC workshop leader

NANCY LAMB

*The Art and Craft of*

# STORYTELLING

*A Comprehensive Guide to*
*Classic Writing Techniques*

**W**
**WRITER'S DIGEST BOOKS**
Cincinnati, Ohio
www.writersdigest.com

For more fine books from F+W Media, visit www.fwmedia.com.

13 12 11 10      6 5 4 3

Distributed in Canada by Fraser Direct, 100 Armstrong Avenue, Georgetown, Ontario, Canada L7G 5S4, Tel: (905) 877-4411. Distributed in the U.K. and Europe by David & Charles, Brunel House, Newton Abbot, Devon, TQ12 4PU, England, Tel: (+44) 1626-323200, Fax: (+44) 1626-323319, E-mail: postmaster@davidandcharles.co.uk. Distributed in Australia by Capricorn Link, P.O. Box 704, Windsor, NSW 2756 Australia, Tel: (02) 4577-3555.

Library of Congress Cataloging-in-Publication Data
Lamb, Nancy.
  The art and craft of storytelling : a comprehensive guide to classic writing techniques / by Nancy Lamb. -- 1st ed.
     p. cm.
  Includes index.
  ISBN 978-1-58297-559-7 (pbk. : alk. paper)
  1. Fiction--Technique. 2. Narration (Rhetoric) I. Title.
  PN3383.N35L36 2008
  808.3--dc22                                          2008032177

Edited by LAUREN MOSKO
Designed by TERRI WOESNER
Cover Designed by CLAUDEAN WHEELER
Production coordinated by MARK GRIFFIN

## DEDICATION

I dedicate this book to all the writers out there who toil in the fields, fueled by little except passion, creativity, and a belief in the dream.

Without artists—without their ability to celebrate life, invent realities, and reveal truths—we would all be diminished. And without art, we would lose our connection to magic.

## ACKNOWLEDGMENTS

My gratitude to Terry Baker and Lia Keyes for their patience in answering my endless questions; and to Ron Alexander, Heather Brown, Max Diamond, Eric Elfman, George Emerson, Troy Fuss, Mary Goodfader, Ethel Gullette, Marianne Jas, Damon Kirsche, Mary Main, Greg Paul Malone, Andrew Martin, Brad Miskell, Ann Paul, Jan Silverstrom-Elfman, and Janet Zarem for their help and insight leavened by humor and intelligence.

I also offer my thanks to the amazing Lauren Mosko, an extraordinary editor whose hard work, sharp eye, and keen intellect made this a better book; and to Jane Friedman, whose open mind made this book possible.

My special thanks to Charles Connor, a stranger who gave me a boost when I needed it most.

Finally, in this electronic age, I must acknowledge Google, Wikipedia, Amazon.com, and Barnesandnoble.com. All four sites offered me a feast of information for my research.

## ABOUT THE AUTHOR

RISING ACTION    CLIMAX    DENOUEMENT

"Denouement" © Greg Paul Malone

Nancy Lamb is the author of forty-three books of fiction and nonfiction for children and adults.

She has taught writing at workshops in Singapore; Athens, Georgia; and Big Sur, California, and is currently working on a new book.

She can be contacted through her Web site, nancylamb.com.

# TABLE OF CONTENTS

# PART I

# BUILDING PLANS

# TIME FRAMES

## Story, Past and Present

---

*Art begins with craft, and there is no art until craft has been mastered.*

—Anthony Burgess

Storytelling is an art. And like any other art, it has rules. Picasso was trained in classical art before he became a cubist. In the beginning, he learned to draw people who looked like people. Once he mastered perspective and line and shading, he could create any number of variations on that portrait by juxtaposing the elements, distorting dimensions, or stacking the third (unseen) dimension on top of the first. Even when he turned his visual world upside down or inside out, he used the fundamentals of his classical training to achieve his goals.

Whether you're writing a fanciful story coaxed from the ether, a memoir pulled from personal experience, or an outasight, never-been-done, experimental novel, the essence of storytelling remains the same. Good story flows from a solid understanding of style and structure along with a confident grasp of character and plot and dialogue. Once you've mastered the fundamentals, you can follow the rules, break the rules, or create new ones. But whatever you do, you will always have a basic foundation to support you.

Throughout your process, the critical thing to remember is to seek the truth of the story. As Picasso said, "Art is a lie that makes us realize truth."

This book deals with fundamentals. We'll look at story ideas and writing and structure. We'll explore what makes a character memorable and what it is about certain stories that makes readers keep turning the pages. We'll talk about beginning, middle, and end; about premise, theme, and tone; about dialogue and point of view; conflict and structure; plot and subplot. We'll examine the importance of choosing a voice that enhances your story as well as the power of using the five senses to add texture and authenticity to that story. And we'll consider how all these elements not only apply to literature, but how they apply to the creation of a published novel, memoir, or screenplay with your name on it.

## THAT WAS THEN

Startled, you wake up in a cave on the side of a rugged ravine. The fading embers of the fire illuminate pictures of bear, bison, and deer painted on rock walls that arch overhead. You hear an ominous growl. Red eyes glare at you in the dim light as you push your infant daughter behind you and grope for the spear. Your fingers tighten around the oak shaft of your weapon as you move into a crouching position. Finding your balance, you raise your arm. Suddenly, the massive shadow lunges toward you, and you hurl the spear. A wild shriek splits the silence of the dawn.

Later that morning, you huddle around a twig-fed fire seeking refuge from the dark of the night. Still trembling, you tell the story of the bear to the people gathered around you. And you tell that tale in breathless detail from beginning to end, describing your terror and your miraculous escape from the jaws of a monster. For in ancient days, when life pulsed with magic and mystery, storytelling commanded a critical place in the life of a clan.

Long before the dawn of the Neolithic era, human beings gathered in small bands in order to enhance their chances of survival. As populations grew, the creative response to the environment—domesticating animals, growing crops, and devising rituals to influence nature—evolved from necessity to inventiveness. This point—around ten thousand years ago, says historian Henry Bamford Parkes—marked the first of four major creative epochs in western civilization.

Parkes speaks of the ancient push-pull between freedom and suppression; that although natural selection favors tribal loyalty and adherence to rules, creativity requires flexibility and freedom. The challenge then—as it is now—was to transcend the constrictions imposed by the tribe in order to invent new ways of thinking and solving problems.

Scholars postulate that spoken language began around 500,000 years ago when hominoids started to hunt large animals. Gestures evolved into sounds that were then assigned meaning by common agreement. Think about it: If you and a friend are fending off a 350-pound cave lion, you've got serious motivation to get your sounds and signals straight.

As human expression evolved from mutual need to common understanding, language took on new meaning, thus sowing the immortal seeds of story. At first, it is supposed, story was used as a teaching tool and as a way to re-tell and re-create exploits and adventures. It then expanded into ritual, historical documentation, and a way of explaining mysterious events. After half a million years of communication, the oral tradition finally evolved into writing.

Close to 4,500 years ago, *The Epic of Gilgamesh* mesmerized Babylonians with tales of the king who was both divine and human. Etched into clay tablets, the stories were written by Shin-eqi-unninni, the first known author in human history to sign his name to his work.

Almost three thousand years ago, the *Iliad* and the *Odyssey*, written by the epic poet Homer, captivated the imaginations of Greeks with tales of the Trojan War. And in early eighth-century England, the exploits of *Beowulf* captured the hearts and minds of Anglo-Saxons. The power of the oral tradition celebrated the *Arabian Nights* and Hamlet and Cinderella, as well as King Arthur and Captain Kidd, Pocahontas and Pancho Villa.

Stories that began as family tales, passed from one generation to the next, were eventually recorded on clay tablets and papyrus, on vellum and paper—priceless gifts from our ancestors.

Throughout history, story has honored our past, enlightened our present, and envisioned our future. Our forebears communicated knowledge, accumulated wisdom, and commemorated common experience through the magic of words. They created myths and entertained crowds. Story has triggered wars and provided building blocks for peace; it has forecast dangers, vilified enemies, and celebrated heroes. And story has also illuminated our common humanity.

## THIS IS NOW

For writers, not much has changed in five millennia. Storytelling still stakes a claim to major portions of our lives. Whether it's books, TV dramas, video games, blogs, or must-see movies, story continues to bring us together in new and ever-evolving ways. Yet, with all this progress over thousands of years of ritual and invention, straddling the gap between the warring factions of tradition and innovation still remains one of the creator's greatest challenges.

As we did then, we look to story for excitement, wisdom, and comfort. And, I believe, we look to story for a connection to our past. Our *ancient* past. Story reaches beyond the written word to create an unconscious continuity with our earliest ancestors, as well as with future generations. And in making these connections, we honor where we came from, who we are, and what we can become.

Helen Keller—blind, deaf, and mute from an illness at the age of eighteen months—learned her first word when she was seven years old. Later, as an adult and noted educator, she described her wordless early world as an "unconscious, yet conscious time of nothingness. I did not know that I knew aught, or that I lived or acted or desired."

It is a privilege to write stories, to give a voice to the voiceless. You open new worlds, you introduce new ways of thinking, and you lift the reader closer to the light. This is the power and purpose of story. And this is the tradition you honor.

## ART AND CRAFT

Some people are born with the gift of storytelling. You know them: friends who can talk about the most mundane encounter and captivate an audience. They know just when to pause, when to draw out the details, and when to deliver the punch line. They've got the instinct for narrative. Even if we're not among those fortunate few blessed with this inherent skill, we can learn how to master it.

Storytelling is an art. But it is also a craft.

Art involves instinct, as well as an appreciation for form and structure. Most of us have that instinct. And if we don't, we can cultivate it.

Craft involves technique. Craft has rules. If a potter doesn't center the clay on the potter's wheel, he can't throw a pot. If a cabinetmaker doesn't measure the wood carefully, cut corners at the proper angle or join those corners correctly, she can't build a level table. What the potter and cabinetmaker produce may be art. But they could not produce that art without craft.

In art and craft—as in this book—it is the process that matters.

# 2

# DISCOVERING YOUR STORY

## The Evocation of the Muse

*In my own judgment, as a reader, the faults of
most novels are the sentences—either they're
ambitious or they're so unclear that they need
to be rewritten. And what's wrong with the
rest of the novels I don't finish is that the
stories aren't good enough to merit writing a
novel in the first place.*

—John Irving

Where do writers get their ideas? How do they pull their stories
out of the ether and give them form? There's no magic formula
here, no right way to create stories, no *only way* to approach
material. There are as many facets to a story as there are people
to imagine it.

The seed of a story often comes from knowledge of something outside yourself; however, it is also possible to recall an
incident from your past that inspires you.

That happened to me. One hot summer day when I was nine years old, my friend Patty was riding her little brother on the back of her bike. He was barefooted. As Patty pedaled down the elm-covered street on her bicycle, her brother's foot brushed against the wheel and—*blech!* you guessed it—the spokes cut off his big toe.

At the same time her brother was being rushed to the emergency room, Patty went in search of the severed toe. After scouring the leafy street, she not only found the toe, she packed it in cotton and saved it in a matchbox.

In no time at all, the toe turned black and wrinkled. Blessed with a generous nature, Patty endeared herself to all the kids in the neighborhood by making her wizened, hidden-under-the-bed trophy available for our rapt inspection whenever we wished—thereby doubling the preadolescent traffic in her house and elevating her status to local legend.

As preposterous as it sounds, my friend Muff Singer and I turned this grisly incident into a wild and crazy children's book called *The World's Greatest Toe Show*, the opening line of which is "The Canal Street Club wouldn't have caused so much trouble if Emily Anderson hadn't saved her father's toe in a matchbox."

Beyond children's books, I've also turned personal tales—both real-life and emotional—into novels. Most writers will confess to the fact that even stories set in places they've never been, from alien planets to Zanzibar, still contain the seeds of personal truth and experience. It's not so much that we write what we know; it's that we write what we feel ... or might have felt.

Almost anything, including severed toes, can be turned into a book. Everyone's life has incidents—comic or tragic, outrageous or ordinary—that contain the seeds of a first-rate story. Finding the way to transform that incident into a compelling narrative, as well as putting it into a viable form that people want to read, is both the challenge and the thrill of writing.

## STRAW INTO GOLD

Just as Rumpelstiltskin spun straw into gold for the miller's daughter, it's our challenge as writers to take the straw we find in our daily lives and weave it into stories that engage the imaginations of readers. One approach is to look for unusual juxtapositions in your daily life—the extraordinary in the ordinary.

I live near the ocean, in Venice, California. A few years ago, I took my dog Max down to the area by the beach to play. It was past ten o'clock at night, and as Max romped and chased balls on the grass, a huge bird swooped close to my head and flew across the bike path to the beach.

I was stunned. It was too big to be a bat. In fact, no large birds fly here at night.

My eyes followed the creature—visible in the glow from the street lamps—as it landed on the post that secured one end of the beach volleyball net.

I walked onto the sand toward it.

The bird didn't move.

I took a few steps closer.

Perched on the volleyball post as if waiting for the game to begin, a horned owl stared straight at me.

I stood there for ten minutes looking at my night visitor. Finally, the owl tired of basking in the glow of human awe. So, with a shrug, he spread his wings and flew into the darkness toward the lifeguard station.

Seeing an owl at the beach is not just unusual, it's outright miraculous. Owls are not beach birds. They are nocturnal creatures that prefer woodlands to ocean. Furthermore, they are not given to hanging around areas where human beings can admire them in the middle of their nightly hunt. That is the only time in my life I have seen an owl that wasn't captured on film, stuffed by a taxidermist, or trapped between the pages of a book.

## LOOKING FOR OWLS IN YOUR OWN LIFE

The owl on the beach is a perfect example of the conjunction of the prosaic and the improbable. These two elements do not belong together—which is precisely what makes them memorable.

We all encounter the extraordinary in the ordinary. It happens all the time. But caught up in the demands of our daily lives, we too often fail to take the time to *see* the extraordinary, to envision it in a story, or to open ourselves to the possibility of mystery.

The owl reminds me that there are lots of ways to use ideas, not the least of which is to seek out unusual combinations and unexpected relationships. Whether these conjunctions occur in your inner life or your outer life—whether they're encountered in a daydream, a car full of kids, or a walk through the produce section at the grocery store—look for those things that fit together even when they don't seem to.

Mark Haddon creates a wonderful example of combining unusual factors in *The Curious Incident of the Dog in the Night-Time*. The hero is Christopher Boone, a fifteen-year-old autistic boy who loves math but can't fathom the minds of people. After he is falsely accused of impaling his neighbor's dog on a pitchfork, Christopher is transformed into a junior Sherlock Holmes as he solves the mystery of the killing. It's startling that a teen who lacks the ability to interpret nuance or grasp the interior lives of others is able to solve a complex mystery of death and deception. But the author combines defect and logic in the character of Christopher and carries off the feat with touching finesse.

As you craft your story, make it a point to experiment with opposites and seek out surprise: Publicly fastidious lawyer has a messy closet; pious church deacon has a gay lover; bucolic setting becomes the home of a serial killer.

Where characters are concerned, that juxtaposition is expressed in the concept of the *shadow*, a hallmark of Jungian psychology that reflects an idea that Plato verbalized 2,500 years ago.

"In all of us," the philosopher wrote, "even in good men, there is a lawless wild-beast nature which peers out in sleep."

Carl Jung called the beast our shadow. Most of us view ourselves as decent people—and we are. But just as Newton's Third Law states that every action has an equal and opposite reaction, every living person has an equal and opposite personality: a light side and a dark side.

The irony is that even though the shadow is ugly and threatening and abhorrent to us, without it we wouldn't be full human beings. Our savage nature not only imbues us with our creativity and passion, it fuels our intuition and inspiration.

Jung believed that the shadow wields extraordinary power over our lives. And to keep this wild-beast nature from getting out of control—from stealing or lying or engaging in violent behavior—it not only needs to be balanced by the strong, healthy part of ourselves, it must be fully acknowledged and integrated into our consciousness.

The problem—and the intrigue—is that most of us behave as if we don't have a shadow. We do this by burying it in the most hidden recesses of our unconscious. Jung understood that not recognizing your shadow can cause serious harm to both yourself and others; that sooner or later it will raise its nasty head from its hiding place and make trouble. Lest you doubt this, just check the news for the latest scandal involving an extramarital affair, a prostitution ring, or political graft. In most instances you'll read about people concealing their sins by publicly accusing others of the very flaw they loathe most in themselves—an excellent way to create a layered character in a story.

Whether we neglect or affirm it, whether we like it or loathe it, our shadow will always be with us. And just like the playground bully, it refuses to be ignored. So, as an author, take advantage of these dichotomies as you create your stories. You'll have more fun writing, and your readers will thank you for your efforts.

## FIND A WAY THAT WORKS

Before we move into how stories are structured and written, I want to reiterate that there is no right or wrong way to write your story. There's no magic formula, no one and only way to accomplish your goals. But there is the accumulated wisdom of thousands of years of storytelling and the collective experience of writers who have walked this path before you.

Ultimately, the best way to write a story is to find a strategy that works for you while honoring the basic conventions and shaping the reader's expectations. Within this context, it's important to understand there are lots of approaches to storytelling, many of which we'll explore in detail. Your most critical goal should be to find a method that fits your temperament, feeds your intellect, and gives you the courage to move forward with confidence and conviction.

# 3

# THE GENRE WARS

## From Romance to Literary Fiction

---

*Books choose their authors; the act of creation is
not entirely a rational and conscious one.*

—Salman Rushdie

For most of the twentieth century, there were five basic forms of fiction: historical, detective, romance, general, and literary. Today, genres—or more accurately, subgenres—are multiplying faster than fleas on a dog. Much of this is due to the hybridization of primary genres. We now have everything from police procedurals and vampire romance to historical thrillers and paranormal fantasy.

Some books, such as Markus Zusak's *The Book Thief* and Shannon Hale's *Austenland*, were marketed to teens, but have sidled into the adult market. Others, like Kaye Gibbons's *Ellen Foster* and J.D. Salinger's *The Catcher in the Rye*, were originally aimed at adults, but have become standard reading fare for teens. And still others, such as the Harry Potter series, were marketed to middle-grade readers and now span multiple generations without breaking stride.

There are few fixed stars in the literary firmament anymore. As soon as Walter Mosley is slotted into the mystery/noir category, he goes off and writes a science-fiction novel. To further complicate the issue, some of his books are quite comfy hanging out on the shelf with serious literary lions. The same paradox applies to Nobel Prize winner Doris Lessing, who began her career writing groundbreaking feminist novels and moved on to science fiction. And then there's the prolific Joyce Carol Oates, who changes genres with every book she creates.

In spite of all this boundary breaking, the reason the categorization of books remains an issue is that most stores shelve their books according to subject or genre. Furthermore, when publishers' representatives sell books to stores, they must identify the books by category and often visit a specific category buyer. Many fine novels have slipped through the cracks because the store and the publisher didn't know how to categorize and market them.

Given the multitude of genres today, this is less likely to happen. Nevertheless, it's imperative to have a working knowledge of what's out there—what the basic expectations are for each genre, and what publishers, editors, and agents handle which kinds of fiction. That will help you position your manuscript to create the strongest possibility of a sale. And it will also help you answer when your agent asks you, "What book/screenplay would you compare your book/screenplay to?"

## CATEGORY BY GENRE

My intention here is not to lock you into fixed categories; rather it is to expose your imagination to storytelling possibilities that help you discover which genre is a comfortable fit with your creative vision.

To get a grasp on where and how your particular story might find a home in such a vast array of categories, this chapter presents an overview of current genres and what the expectations are for each.

Note: If you're interested in more detail on the different genres, you can find an extensive list of books that represent each category in the appendix.

## General Fiction

### Expectations

*General fiction* is the catchall name for the well-told story that doesn't find a fit in the other genres. Here, readers expect that the book be a "good read," that it be compelling, either psychologically or emotionally. It should also open up worlds and minds, events and relationships, for our sustained voyeuristic pleasure.

Because the genre itself is so fluid, nothing fits perfectly here. For instance, chick lit began in the romance category. But after becoming so pervasive, it sashayed right into general fiction and never looked back. Lesbian and gay lit has also expanded beyond its original niche category and is staking a claim in the mainstream literary landscape.

### Categories

- **Chick lit:** Stories that feature a protagonist, usually in her twenties or thirties, coping with love, career, and identity in the modern world. The tone is traditionally upbeat, offering readers a hopeful, if not happy, ending.

- **Domestic drama:** This includes anything and everything from the death of a child, to the infidelities of a spouse, to the trials of being a single parent.

- **Sports:** From team sports to golf, stories dramatized on playing fields, in locker rooms, in bars, and in the personal lives of protagonists and antagonists.

- **Vampire lit:** Bram Stoker's *Dracula* started the craze in the late nineteenth century, and Anne Rice's *Interview With the Vampire* updated the tradition for the twentieth century. The stories usually involve the living and the sharp-toothed "undead" clashing in the real world.

- **LGBT (Lesbian, Gay, Bisexual, Transgender) lit:** Life, love, and romance played out against a primary backdrop of gay communities throughout the western world. The stories often involve the idea of the hero reclaiming ownership of his or her identity.

- **Humor:** From acid satire to funny ha-ha, stories that make you smile and—at their best—even laugh out loud. The most memorable ones manage to mine humor from tragedy and create satire out of reality.

- **War stories:** Chronicles of conflict—usually historical, from ancient Greeks to contemporary battles—laden with enemies and leavened by heroes.

- **Mélange:** This is the catchall for stories that don't fit easily in other categories. It includes everything from sex, drugs, and rock 'n' roll to comedy, tragedy, and standard drama.

## Historical Fiction

### Expectations

Historical fiction readers love to learn while they read great stories. Fans demand that the history be accurate and full of period detail. If the book isn't imbued with a texture true to the times, it will be shunted aside for more enthralling reads. Furthermore, if historical characters are woven into the plot, their stories should be based on solid research and embellished with action that's a plausible outgrowth of known facts.

The only limiting factor in these genres is the writer's imagination. If you have a passion for Roman history or have developed an affinity for the American West, use your interests to create a living, breathing setting for your story.

### Categories

- **Romance:** Some of these stories involve royalty, others have just plain folks, and the conflict is often steeped in conventions of the historical period; the commonality is that no obstacle is too great to overcome when true love is at stake.

- **Detective thriller:** Mysteries that feature innovative ways to track down and identify the perp when there weren't fingerprints to match, DNA databases to search, and photographs to peruse.

- **Adventure:** Dramas played out on high seas and dry land—sometimes based on real historical events and sometimes set in challenging places involving obstacles or enemies to overcome and battles to be waged.

- **Family saga:** Families past and present hand down gifts and curses from one generation to the next, surviving crises, causing conflicts, creating rifts, and inviting reconciliation.

- **Drama:** Personal dramas generally set against large backdrops, such as wars, crises, and heroic quests. Some stories also focus on inner torment and outer conflicts.

- **Multi-volume historical saga:** Stories of love, drama, and conflict played out by the same characters—or the heirs of those characters—in several volumes.

## Romance

### *Expectations*

Blame it on Jane. *Emma, Pride and Prejudice, Sense and Sensibility*—Jane Austen's books set the standard for all the romance novels that have followed over the last two hundred years.

As Austen knew instinctively, readers of romance novels want to read about love. And they want a happy ending. (Don't we all?) Here, more than in any other genre, the focus of the story is on relationship: how it forms and how it works out. The relationship drama is grounded in the thrill of the chase. The heroine must overcome untold obstacles—including a major clash of wills between the woman and her intended—before she ends up with the man of her dreams. And because the audience for the books is unabashedly female (with the exception of gay romance novels), the stories are told from the woman's point of view.

For most of the twentieth century, romance novels were confined to the stereotypical bodice ripper—beautiful woman with heaving bosom falls for elusive man with throbbing thighs. But with the burgeoning of this genre, subcategories have replicated faster than a dashing gentleman can rescue a damsel in distress. The latest iterations on the romance theme are NASCAR romance and erotic romance. But it won't stop there. Romance novels represent a multibillion-dollar business. And as long as there are writers to write them, publishers will be eager to publish them.

## Categories

- **Creatures of the night:** Often involves a vampire or werewolf falling for someone outside the clan. The question then becomes, "To bite or not to bite?" The conflict includes the dilemma of whether to step into the dark side or give up love and remain "human."

- **Historical romance:** Whether it's in the midst of pirates, wars, or Vikings, men and women meet, separate, and meet again in settings that predate World War II. The heroines are usually stronger and more educated than the typical woman of the period.

- **Regency romance:** A subset of historical romance, these novels tell of love and intrigue in early nineteenth-century England, around the time of Jane Austen's novels.

- **Paranormal romance:** The settings can be anything from other worldly to serious psychic to science fiction. The point is to create the romantic push-pull in fantastical places.

- **LGBT romance:** Men falling in love with men, women falling in love with women—conflicts, combinations, and permutations played out in the multifaceted world of gay life.

- **Inspirational romance:** Using Christianity as a backdrop, the romances are filled with desire and restrained by chastity. There is no sex until after marriage, but there is a celebration of fidelity, forgiveness, and redemption.

- **Contemporary romance:** Post-World War II stories that feature feisty heroines with contemporary values and meaningful work. The racier ones fall under the category of erotic romance.

## Mysteries and Thrillers

### Expectations

According to Terry Baker—a writer and former owner of Mystery Annex at Small World Books in Venice, California—there is one no-exceptions rule for this genre: Mysteries and thrillers must be page-turners. Readers of this genre demand a fast-moving plot filled with accurate, intriguing detail.

And they also appreciate "insider" information, such as learning crime-scene investigation techniques to track a cryptic clue to find the killer. And speaking of clues, in mysteries and thrillers (or in any other genre, for that matter), the author is not allowed to introduce a solution whose clue was not presented earlier in the novel. Whether the reference is hidden in plain sight or dropped beneath a pile of rubble, the clue must be acknowledged in some way before the solution to the mystery is revealed.

Finally, Baker says that the lure of fiction (mystery or otherwise) for the armchair traveler is significant. It's a good point to keep in mind when you're choosing a setting for your story.

These categories, too, have expanded with the times. In fact, they've exploded. Police dramas, whodunits, and amateur sleuths no longer claim exclusive rights to mysteries and thrillers. You can check the appendix for a roundup of usual suspects.

## Categories

- **Detectives:** Amateur and professional sleuths—from private eyes to bounty hunters—track down the bad guys, placing themselves in imminent danger in the process.

- **Cozy:** Mysteries set in a gentler world, involving amateurs—usually ladies—solving crimes in small towns or intimate settings where ingenuity trumps serious forensic tools.

- **Christian:** Mysteries solved within and around the ethos of Christian values.

- **Noir:** The protagonist isn't necessarily a detective; it can be someone directly involved in a crime story that's peppered with dark designs, serious sex, and gritty detail.

- **Forensic:** Coroners and medical examiners, male and female, search for answers to crimes in bullets, bugs, and bodies.

- **Police procedural:** Here, the solution is in the details of how police detectives follow leads and solve crimes. Often the perp is known from the outset, and it's up to the police to prove this is the bad guy.

- **Courtroom/legal:** In this subgenre, evidence is everything. The drama ultimately plays out in a courtroom filled with good guys and bad guys, each trying to get the best of the other.

- **LGBT mystery:** Whodunits with a same-sex twist played out in settings around the world. The stories are usually contemporary in both ethos and action.

- **Historical:** From the Middle Ages to the middle of the twentieth century, mystery and drama wrapped in an aura of the era and steeped in detail and logic.

- **Thriller:** Roller-coaster rides transposed to the page as good and evil meet face-to-face.

- **Ghost story:** Shadows, specters, and spirits—both "real" and imagined—send chills down the spines of the most stalwart characters ... not to mention the readers.

- **Horror:** Hard-core horror, with liberal doses of violence and terror mixed into edge-of-your-seat plots.

- **Spy:** Post-World War II stories with roots in the past that feature spies going after bad guys and encountering peril in the process.

## Science Fiction

### Expectations

When I asked my local expert, Heather Brown—a science fiction and fantasy maven raised in the shadow of Small World Books in Venice, California—to define the difference between science fiction and fantasy, she opined that the two can be metaphorically divided between lasers and swords. I would add that science fiction has multitudinous subcategories, while fantasy's borders seem more porous.

In science fiction, the world is envisioned in high-tech, which often sets up a power struggle between man and machine. Furthermore, the expectation is that even though the stories explore unknown worlds, they should be grounded in known elements of science—the reason, no doubt, that theoretical physicists and other scientists are drawn to writing science fiction.

Readers want to be taken out of this world and transported to unfamiliar terrain—the more unfamiliar, the better. In science fiction, as Brown says, "there are no boundaries to the possible."

Like mysteries and thrillers, the categories of science fiction are crossbreeds and mongrels, limited only by the writer's imagination.

### Categories

- **Soft science fiction:** Humans suffering human dilemmas while interacting with inhuman elements beyond their ken.

- **Apocalypse and postapocalypse:** Devastation—nuclear, environmental, cataclysmic—is visited on humans trying to survive the bleak wreckage of a new and dangerous age.

- **Cyberpunk:** Loners living amidst the ruins of dystopic landscapes—usually urban—in which secret implants, dangerous information, and technology have spun out of control.

- **Feminist science fiction:** Gender roles—stereotypical and not—explored in alien surroundings and under challenging circumstances.

- **Comic science fiction:** Authors take known elements and skew them into twisted circumstances—both mechanical and human—that draw humor from human longing and frailty.

- **First contact:** That moment in time when humans first encounter alien societies and what happens when the two cultures try to get along—or not.

- **Colonization:** Like pioneers moving to the wild, wild West, humans colonize and create new civilizations where war and peace are part of life.

- **Military science fiction:** Humans—mostly men—battle out-of-control aliens, machines, and the elements in a race to survive the challenges of a hostile universe.

- **Time travel:** Tales of humans crossing the space-time continuum—accidentally or on purpose—into both the past and the future as they cope with the unanticipated joys and horrors of living in new worlds.

- **Steampunk:** Adventures in a fantastical alternate Victorian-era with "advanced technology," such as clockwork computers and rocket ships powered by steam.

- **Hard science fiction:** Stories usually concocted by men and women whose non-writing profession is theoretical physics, astrophysics, and other intellectual pursuits connected with serious science.

# Fantasy

## Expectations

Here, myth and legend take center stage as they forge the hero's journey. The story at the heart of fantasy is the glorification of the human spirit dramatized through conflict. That conflict may include any combination of mythological and fairy-tale props, creatures, and customs—elves, faeries, monsters, dragons, ogres, wars, castles, romance, spells, magic, quests, and other original or time-tested elements.

In fantastical worlds, there are rules to be followed and a mission to be accomplished. The heroes (human or otherwise) are often lost, abandoned, or cast out into the world alone. Furthermore, they have something—a sword, a scar, a ring ... even leprosy—that sets them apart from their fellow beings.

On the journey toward fulfillment, the hero experiences triumph, failure, and power on a mythical scale. The hero's experience usually ends in the quest fulfilled. But in the hands of a master such as J.R.R. Tolkien, triumph is shaded by a tragic flaw. In *The Lord of the Rings*, Frodo's quest is accomplished—but not by his own hand. Frodo fails as a hero in the end because his craving for power overcomes his desire to make the honorable decision. And in one single act, he falls from grace—thus becoming a moral and emotional failure.

A fantasy aficionado friend of mine says the exploration of the shadow is also evident in this genre; that fantasy is often used as an allegory to offer a fresh perspective on existing problems in our own world. It also feeds the need for the spiritual in those who can't find it in religion.

## Categories

This is a group in which genres blend and crossbreed to such an extent that each stands on its own—yet is often inspired by archetypical predecessors. Furthermore, because of the genre's inbred nature, it's often difficult to distinguish one category from another.

Fantasy has had lots of iterations over the years. Yet the appetite for these stories seems insatiable, and they are frequently transformed into movies and TV productions, along with computer games and graphic novels. Whether they take place on distant planets, in alien societies, or in the here and now, contemporary stories are usually grounded in settings that echo elements of the Middle Ages.

In this genre, technology takes a back seat to magic and mystery. Dwarves, faeries, and elves often interact with humans in a "normal" way. Here, the stories unfold in an eclectic mix of many genres, yet each has a distinctive aura.

Although the stories mix and match with ease, here's a general overview of some of the hybrids you might expect to find in this category.

- **Heroic fantasy:** From Homer's *Odyssey* to Joyce's *Ulysses* to *Star Wars*, the hero's journey laid out in classical form.

- **Arthurian legend:** The epic tale of the young king who must rise to meet his destiny never grows old in the imagination of storytellers.

- **Dark fantasy:** These stories are kissing cousins of horror, but aren't as ugly or as graphic in their detail.

- **Urban fantasy:** Real-world urban settings transformed by paranormal elements into new "realities" created in the crucible of conflict.

- **Alternate history:** "What if this had happened instead of that?" is placed in a context in which real historical characters intersect with magic, often in a way that is considered "normal."

- **Role-playing games (RPGs):** The reader/players assume the identity of fictional characters as they use preset rules to make their way through dangerous and challenging worlds.

- **High fantasy:** It's good against evil in worlds constructed in epic proportions; often, the fate of people and nations hangs in the balance between victory and defeat.

- **Science fantasy:** This is a blend of fantasy with science or pseudoscience, in which something like genetic engineering is used to explain the existence of dragons. As Rod Serling said, "Science fiction makes the implausible possible, while science fantasy makes the impossible plausible."

## Autobiography and Memoir

### *Expectations*

When St. Augustine wrote his classic memoir, *The Confessions of St. Augustine*, around 398 A.D., he started a self-revelatory trend that has yet to end. His thirteen-book series—part memoir, part autobiography—chronicles his life from infancy through his wild and crazy youth to his eventual conversion to Christianity and subsequent reflections on the meaning of his religious convictions.

A thousand years later in England, the mystic Julian of Norwich penned her story, *Sixteen Revelations of Divine Love*. Believed to be the first book written by a woman in the English language, her memoir adopts an optimistic (and some say, more feminized) concept of God—a deity who is compassionate and mysterious and a source of infinite grace.

After her touching story, we were momentarily mired in *Grace Abounding to the Chief of Sinners*, a seventeenth-century memoir by John Bunyan, in which he confesses to such unforgivable sins as indulging in profane language, dancing, and bell ringing. (Bunyan is also the author of *The Pilgrim's Progress*, possibly the most tedious novel ever written in the English language.) Eventually, memoir sailed across the Atlantic to the New World, where Frederick Douglass wrote *Narrative of the Life of Frederick Douglass: An American Slave* in 1845.

Since that time, memoirs have been written by people of every class and belief system, with every conceivable life experience, throughout the globe. As a consequence, we have been privileged to enter the lives and psyches of some extraordinary people, both familiar and unfamiliar, good and evil.

As I see it, the difference between autobiography and memoir is that the former is a more factual accounting of one's life and the latter is an accounting passed through the filters of memory, emotion, and reflection. Also, memoir usually encompasses one period of a person's life, not the life story from beginning to end.

The yearning for self-expression burns in the hearts of most artists. Memoirs and autobiographies are born from passion and a longing to give voice to thoughts and emotions normally confined to our psyches.

Memoirs that stand the test of time are more than a snapshot of an event in a life; they are stories of struggle or triumph, of what it's like to be rich and famous or reduced to living on the street. Occasionally, they are also a reflection on, or rationalization for, stupid or shameful behavior. Here, reader expectations are grounded in the drama. Readers want to be inspired, to be shown how to cope and how to overcome. Often the message we take away from a memoir is "if she can do it, so can I"—a message that never seems to wear out its welcome.

The other attribute we distill from most successful memoirs is a fundamental concept of what Ernest Hemingway called "grace under pressure"—the personal quality he cited as the singular hallmark of the hero. Most of these authors manage to tell their tales without crying victim or wallowing in pity puddles, which makes their stories even more memorable. It's worth noting that standout memoirs are often made into movies dubbed "biopics." This is, I believe, because the stories evoke a sense of awe that these amazing events could actually happen to someone.

The fact is, the majority of us haven't led lives that contain the drama necessary to create a bestseller. But if you *are* inhabiting one of those lives, go for it.

And the rest of us? We continue to pilfer our past, searching for truths that can be recast on the pages of our next novel.

## Categories

Autobiographies and memoirs are as varied as their authors. Nevertheless, it's possible to sort them by type.

- **Boot strap:** Up-from-the-gutter stories that demonstrate the indomitable spirit of extraordinary men and women who often think of themselves as ordinary.

- **Political:** Memoirs written to uncover and illuminate the lives and actions of intriguing people.

- **Family:** If your mother beat you, your father seduced you, or your family was caught in tragic or dramatic circumstances, the story has the potential to become classic family memoir. No normal families need apply.

- **Celebrity:** From comic to serious, famous people tell famous and infamous stories about their lives and the people they have known.

- **Travel:** Escape, revelation, and sometimes redemption discovered in foreign cultures and countries.

- **Survival:** From war and isolation to courage and improvisation, harrowing stories of fearsome circumstances survived against all odds.

- **Extraordinary lives:** Here, you meet the heroes—memorable men and women who find a way to triumph over some of fate's cruelest blows.

- **Confession and conversion:** Books often written with an eye to redeeming, revising, or refurbishing the public image of a person who lived in—and perhaps influenced—challenging times.

- **Spiritual memoir:** Sin, searching, and redemption played out amidst personal quest and spiritual longing.

- **Writer's memoir:** Writers train both comedic and serious eyes on a period of their lives marked by struggle, revelation, and insight.

# New Journalism

## *Expectations*

This genre came of age in the 1960s and 1970s, when experimentation (be it with psychedelic drugs or narrative style) was the norm.

In contrast to standard journalistic practices in which the reporter maintains his distance from the subject and is absent from the story, in this new form of writing, the reporter becomes a major player—if not the star—of the narrative. In fact, it was not uncommon for the reporter to convey the story from a first-person point of view.

Besides playing with voice and perspective, this type of narrative nonfiction adopts other elements of fiction writing. The traditional "inverted pyramid" format of newspaper stories is rejected, and emphasis is placed on the *story*, complete with vivid dialogue, developed scenes, digressions, editorial asides, flashbacks, foreshadowing, and other fictive techniques. (Think of Hunter S. Thompson's *Fear and Loathing in Las Vegas*, which was much more a story of his drug-addled adventures and "the search for the American Dream" than it was the Mint 400 desert race he was sent to cover for a major sports magazine.)

## *Categories*

Rather than being broken into multiple subgenres, the stories in this genre fit under one inclusive and multicolored literary umbrella. Their unifying element is the use of a personal point of view to report on events, which distinguishes them from traditional journalism.

# Literary Fiction

## *Expectations*

There are scads of definitions of literary fiction. But the basic understanding is that the genre pays special attention to prose style, tone, and linguistic craft while tackling a serious or epic subject—even if the tackle is accomplished in a comedic or satiric way. These books also demonstrate an original creative vision and are ostensibly more intellectually demanding than mainstream commercial fiction. (Sometimes, however, what appears on the surface to be "intellectual" is, in fact, mere pretension.) Above all, literary fiction demonstrates a depth and substance that makes these books classics in every sense of the word.

This genre tends to be seen in artistic opposition to detective fiction, thrillers, science fiction, romance, and fantasy. That said, there are lots of exceptions to this rule—Kurt Vonnegut's *Slaughterhouse-Five*, Philip Pullman's *His Dark Materials* trilogy, and Walter Mosley's *Devil in a Blue Dress* spring to mind.

### Categories

Basically, this is just one ever-expanding category. There's lots of wiggle room for the author as long as the book is well crafted and well written. The stories can be historical or contemporary, science fiction or saga. In fact, "literary" defies categorization, which is why you'll see a combined reading list, without subcategories, in the appendix.

## YOUR PERSONAL AIMS

As you probably know, different agents and editors often have distinct preferences for the kinds of books they handle. Some consider any project, while others are drawn to specific areas, such as mysteries or memoirs or fantasies.

Before you start writing—let alone worrying about pitching your book to an editor or agent—take the time to do your reading homework and understand the genre you're interested in. Ask yourself:

- What kind of book do I want to write?

- How does it compare with other books in this genre?

- What about a subgenre?

- Are there certain rules I should adhere to in order for my book to be classified in a certain way?

- What are my book's strongest assets and how can I use them to the best advantage when I present my manuscript to agents and editors?

As I've said before, my intent isn't to lock you into one specific way of thinking about storytelling. The goal is to open your mind to possibilities so that your book intrigues a publisher and fulfills its promise to an enthusiastic reading audience.

# PART II

# FOUNDATION AND STRUCTURE

# 4

# STRUCTURAL DESIGN
## Building What Works for You

---

*Structure is nothing more than a way of looking at your story material so that it's organized in a way that's both logical and dramatic.*

—Jack M. Bickham

Structure isn't a prefabricated box you cram your story into. It is a flexible framework that helps you move through your narrative without losing your way.

Think of structure as a series of road signs posted along the journey of your story. Think also of structure as the rails that keep you from straying onto meandering paths that so often lure a writer from the true course of a story.

Structure creates the underpinning of the book. Without it, narrative has no form and plot has no provocative way to move the reader from one moment to the next—from one scene to the next.

The most basic element of structure is what we were all taught in school: beginning, middle, and end. If there is a fixed star in the universe of storytelling, this is it. Every story has a beginning, middle, and end. Every scene has a beginning, middle, and end. But how these elements are dramatized—how they are conceived and shaped, juxtaposed and presented—is up to you.

Storytelling rules aren't restrictions. In fact, a basic understanding of the rules frees you to do your job as a writer. Again, think of Picasso and how his true-to-life lithographs and etchings from the 1920s informed his later work.

As I said earlier, there is no one perfect way to fit the puzzle pieces of a story together in order to create a viable dramatic whole. Each author must approach the structuring of a story in a way that feels comfortable for him or her. The attainment of this goal doesn't happen overnight. Developing one single story often requires experimenting and planning and falling on your literary ass more than once before you find the way that works for your particular narrative. The most important issue is to keep on trying until you get it right. And you can get it right if you find the structure that suits your psyche, your vision, and your temperament.

## EIGHT APPROACHES TO STRUCTURING YOUR STORY

As you've no doubt gathered by now, I'm not a fan of a my-way-or-the-highway approach to narrative. Rules are made, if not to be broken, then at least to be bent. With that in mind, here are eight different approaches for structuring your story. Try them on. Experiment. If you don't find something that fits, create your own literary wardrobe—keeping in mind that what makes sense to you should also make sense to your reader.

### I. Keep It Simple

The most fundamental way to look at story is as a narrative with a beginning, middle, and end. Formulate what each of these means to the plot and how they relate to each other. Then write your story.

- In the beginning, define what your hero wants and why he wants it.

- In the middle, create the obstacles the hero must overcome in order to accomplish his goal.

- In the end, resolve the situation in a believable and logical way.

Once you've settled on these fundamentals in your own mind, build a story around them, expanding each section and enlarging each plot point as you move through the narrative.

Beginning, middle, and end: the mind, heart, and soul of story.

## 2. Play It As It Lays

Make a few notes about your characters and scenes. Get a firm concept in your head of what your book is about. Then take a deep breath and begin.

Here, you're winging it, allowing one situation to lead to the next that leads to the next. There's not much advance planning here. But there is room for spontaneity.

For most authors—even seasoned ones—this is a risky way to write a book. The open-ended approach makes it too easy to stray from a well-plotted story path. That said, there's no question this improvisational method works for some people. Playing it as it lays is analogous to walking down a dark and unfamiliar road using only a tiny flashlight. You can't see far in front of you, but if you focus carefully on the business at hand, it's possible to make it all the way to the end of the road without stumbling.

In this approach, begin by putting your hero in the opening situation and presenting the opening complication. Then, let your characters do the talking and your imagination do the walking.

Finally, as you stroll down the path from beginning to end, keep in mind the rules of the road that you were taught as a child.

- "Stop" to analyze what actions your characters choose or are thrust into by circumstance.

- "Look" at what your characters do, staying open to the subconscious meaning of their actions and reactions.

- "Listen" to what your characters have to say, taking advantage of the implications of their dialogue on the page and their whispers in your ear.

When you approach a story in this evolutionary fashion, your ability to access your unconscious and to honor your imagination plays a major role in the creative process.

## 3. Take Baby Steps

If dealing with the challenges of plot is daunting to you, break your story into manageable segments that remove the intimidation from the task. Establish the primary story elements of beginning, middle, and end. Once you've done this, envision your narrative as an ongoing, interconnected chain of scene and sequel. One action causes a reaction that causes another action and reaction. Step by step, scene by sequel, you construct one progression after another, shaping a story—from simple to complex—with these basic building blocks of plot.

For instance, after you open your scene, ask yourself the following questions:

- What is the logical sequel to this scene?

- What action does this scene trigger that leads to the next scene?

- How have I planted the hook to pull the reader into the next scene?

- What has my hero done to move the story along?

- How does this scene contribute to the larger context of the book?

Using this step-by-step method, you move through your story from the beginning through the middle to the end.

## 4. Create a Literary Outline

Many of us were taught in school how to outline written assignments—starting with Roman numerals, then moving on to A. B. C., 1. 2. 3., a. b. c., and so forth. You can break down the plot of a book in the same way. Once you've blocked out the story, follow the clearly marked trail you've set out for yourself from one chapter to the next, from beginning to end.

Although your outline is an integral part of the structure, you needn't consider it a fixed entity. Don't be afraid to make changes or explore a new possibility when characters lead you down a different path.

Before you write the book, break down each chapter into a basic outline form, noting which characters and situations are involved in each chapter. You don't need to be too detailed. The purpose of the outline is to provide a map for you to follow and give you an overview of the book. Furthermore, it's not necessary to plot out every twist and turn in the road; some of the most interesting journeys involve sudden detours and un-expected encounters. Even as you follow the map, make every effort to stay open to surprise.

## 5. Walk the North Forty

Develop a detailed chapter-by-chapter diagram of your book, creating a visual map for you to follow. Once you grasp this overview, you'll have a stronger picture of what is happening in your story. When you see those places where you have dropped a plot stitch or where one character hasn't appeared in a while, you can pick up the thread before you move on.

I began writing my first novel without a plan. But it soon became evident that I needed a structural guide for my loosely conceived story. With the help of my friend Terry Baker, I constructed a running chart of my book, laid out and orga-nized on shelf paper. A lengthy visual aid, to say the least. But it worked.

First I divided the paper into chapter sections with a verti-cal line. I did the same thing for characters, plot, and subplots in horizontal lines that intersected the chapters. I then marked down the appearances of the various characters in different col-ored inks throughout the grid. One character was blue. One was red. Another was green. I did the same thing for the plot lines—making notes here and there as reminders that I shouldn't forget to include these things in the book.

When I finally rolled out the plot diagram—all twelve feet of it—across my living room floor and took a look at it, my entire novel was laid out before me in living color.

In order to get a sense of what was happening in the book, I strolled the length of my outline like a rancher checking the fence on the north forty. I looked for plot and character omissions. I examined my overlaps and excesses—most of which were immediately apparent after inspecting the chart. If there were no red or green or blue notations for two chapters, I could see that I had to remind the reader about this character or pick up the thread of that subplot. If the plot was dominated by one color, I re-examined the balance I had created between characters.

This strategy can apply to fiction and nonfiction, short books and long ones. In fact, I've used variations on this approach for several of my books. And each time I do it I gain comfort and confidence from the concrete visualization the chart provides.

## 6. Decorate Your Wall

Make scene-by-scene notes on 3×5 cards and arrange them on a wall or bulletin board. The advantage of this method is that you can change your cards around, add some and toss others, without messing up your overall story.

If a bulletin board is too confining, choose a door or a blank wall. Then use Post-it notes to define characters and create scenes. Not only do these notes come in different colors, they also come in different sizes. Take advantage of the variety.

As in the visual-mapping method above, color-coding characters and plot helps you clarify your story. Once you have the visual of the whole, you can see what character or theme or plot point is missing.

## 7. Use Classical Structure

Follow classical story structure of Greek drama from the inciting incident to the climax to the resolution. Whether you're writing the story of a quest or puzzling through the challenges of an experimental novel, this method offers a time-tested way to formulate your story.

We'll examine classical drama in detail in chapter nine. This method walks hand in hand with the Hero Quest covered in chapter twelve.

## 8. Mix and Match

Do your own thing. Consider all the different ways to structure your narrative, and then choose the methods you prefer. If you want to mix scene and sequel with a literary map, do it. There are no rules here. Your goal should be to find the combination that is the most effective for your psyche, as well as your story.

Keep in mind that none of these approaches are carved in stone. You've got lots of options and room to move. As I said before, the best way to structure your story is what works for you. That means you should trust in your story, honor the fundamental conventions of plot and structure, and promise yourself you'll finish what you set out to do.

## STRUCTURAL DESIGN: COMBINATIONS AND PERMUTATIONS

As you structure the story you're working on, ask yourself what type of person you are: a fly-by-the-seat-of-your-pants type, or a take-control-and-eliminate-surprises type?

If you're the improv type, organize your book using suggestions 1, 2, or 3.

If you're one of those people with "control issues," organize your book using suggestions 4, 5, 6, or 7.

If more than one approach appeals to you, try number 8.

This is the time to experiment. If one approach isn't a good fit, try another. As you try these out, ask yourself:

- Which method gives me the most confidence in writing my story?

- Which method do I feel the most comfortable using?

- Which plan allows me to move from beginning to end with the most ease?

- Which approach offers me the greatest chance of finishing my book?

Don't be afraid to commit to a technique and start writing your book. But if you get stuck, don't be afraid to make a change. Experiment until you find an approach to structure that suits your temperament, gives you courage, and fuels your creativity.

## 5

# BREAKING GROUND

## How to Begin the Beginning

---

*Every storyteller is in the expectations-
management business and must take
responsibility for leading listeners effectively
through the story experience, incorporating
both surprise and fulfillment.*

—Peter Guber

A practical fact: If you don't capture an editor's interest at the beginning of a story, it's unlikely you'll have that editor's attention for the rest of the book. At the most, you've got two or three pages to hook the reader. Whether you're writing a screenplay or a novel, that is a writer's reality. Especially a first-time writer's reality.

With rare exceptions, you must accomplish storytelling magic immediately or your manuscript will be tossed onto the paper mountain or into the electronic trashcan commonly referred to as the Rejection Pile. You will then receive a polite form letter from the editor or producer informing you that the story you've slaved over for three years is "not right for our list" or "doesn't fit our needs at this time."

Every writer I know—published and unpublished—is painfully familiar with variations on this literary kiss-off.

It won't matter that pages 10 to 450 of your story are some of the most compelling ever written in the annals of literature. Chances are those pages won't be read as long as they are preceded by a weak beginning.

That said, do your best to create a dynamite opening. As Seattle librarian Nancy Pearl said on National Public Radio, "I think when you read a good first line, it's like falling in love with somebody."

A survey conducted in Great Britain for Costa (which sponsors the prize formerly known as the Whitbread Book Award, for the most enjoyable book of the year) confirms this fact. It found that 43 percent of readers know by the end of the first chapter whether they will finish a book. One third of the readers know by the time they read fifty pages.

Television and the Internet have shortened attention spans and made us more impatient readers and viewers. What worked fifty years ago doesn't necessarily work now. There are notable exceptions, of course. But this does not change the fact that if you don't hook the reader at the opening, you run the risk of the reader moving on to—and buying—another book.

An intriguing beginning anchors the story in the imagination of the reader by presenting a powerful need to know what happens next. It also gives the writer a handle on the narrative, both present and future.

## TRICKS OF THE TRADE
### Finding the Perfect First Line

If you think you've written a terrific first scene but feel it still lacks punch, scan the first few pages of your story and read the first line of each paragraph. Writers often spin their wheels for a few paragraphs or pages, setting the scene and filling in background before they dive into the action.

Look for a line that pops off the page—a possible opening line that will hook the reader even though there's no set-up for the information disclosed. Maybe it's a snippet of dialogue or something mysterious. The reader doesn't need an immediate explanation—what he needs is a hook. If you discover a line that shocks the reader to attention, use it. You can always provide the background information later.

## FROM ANCIENT GREECE TO DEEP SPACE

In classical drama, the Greeks called the opening scene the *inciting incident*. This is the dramatic action that triggers the *rising motion*—the initial complication of the plot—and propels your story from the beginning through the middle to the end.

The inciting incident is the catalyst for your entire story because it sets up the conflict of opposing interests: This is what your hero wants; this is why she can't have it. If the inciting incident is not powerful enough, your plot won't have the necessary momentum to sustain the reader's interest.

Imagine that your story is a spaceship preparing to take off for a journey to the moon. This particular trip has three distinct parts analogous to beginning, middle, and end: the movement through the Earth's atmosphere, the travel across open space, and the landing on the moon.

Science dictates that a spaceship cannot travel out of the Earth's atmosphere to its final destination if the booster rockets aren't powerful enough to thrust it beyond Earth's gravitational pull. For instance, the designated escape velocity for planet Earth is 25,000 miles per hour. If a spaceship fails to reach this speed, it will founder and fall, then burn into embers.

With that disaster scenario in mind, think of your opening—your inciting incident—as the booster rockets that must contain enough power to drive the reader past the beginning. Then construct your story accordingly.

## EIGHT CONSIDERATIONS FOR THE OPENING GAMBIT

In today's climate of short attention spans and electronic distractions, it's more important than ever to capture the reader's attention right from the beginning of your story. You can do this with a whimper or a bang. The goal is to grab hold of your reader's imagination in a compelling way and to maintain that connection from beginning to end.

Here are eight strategies to keep in mind when you write your opening paragraph. You can use one or two of these techniques, or you can use all of them. The choice is up to you.

### 1. Offer a Taste of the Book

Give the reader a sense of what the book is about by introducing the tone, the conflicts, and possibly the theme.

For example, look at how Philip Roth conveys a sense of the story in the opening of *Portnoy's Complaint*:

> She was so deeply imbedded in my consciousness that for the first year of school I seem to have believed that each of my teachers was my mother in disguise. As soon as the last bell had sounded, I would rush off for home, wondering as I ran if I could possibly make it to our apartment before she had succeeded in transforming herself. Invariably she was already in the kitchen by the time I arrived, and setting out my milk and cookies.

What information is revealed here? How do you know what the book is about? In two sentences, we know this kid has "issues" with his mother. Serious issues, as it turns out. We also know that this is a writer who injects a hint of humor into his prose.

The character tension, combined with an appealing voice, is enough to hook us into this book. (And, of course, after the novel was first published, one famously shocking scene became the talk of the nation—an excellent way to send the book to the top of the best-seller list.)

## 2. Reveal a Problem

Some books state the problem right up front. Others just hint at it. Either way, the reader is successfully pulled into the unfolding human drama.

Scott Turow's *Personal Injuries* opens with:

> He knew it was wrong, and that he was going to get caught. He said he knew this day was coming.
>
> He knew they had been stupid, he told me—worse, greedy. He said he knew he should have stopped. But somehow, each time he thought they'd quit, he'd ask himself how once more could make it any worse. Now he knew he was in trouble.
>
> I recognized the tune. Over twenty-some years, the folks sitting in that leather club chair in front of my desk have found only a few old standards in the jukebox. I Didn't Do It. The Other One Did It. Why Are They Picking On Me. His Selection, I'm Sorry, made the easiest listening. But they all wanted to hear the same song from me: Maybe I Can Get You Out Of This.

Like Roth, the author weaves his own brand of humor into the prose, a quiet wit that lurks just offstage. At the same time, Turow injects a note of seriousness into the opening. By the time a potential reader finishes the first page, he's hooked. He wants to know what the criminal did and if he's going to get out of this bind.

## 3. Reveal Character

Sometimes revelation is accomplished in a subtle way, with the author hinting at the kind of person the hero is. Other times the emotional state of the protagonist is apparent from the opening sentence.

In J.D. Salinger's *The Catcher in the Rye*, Holden Caulfield—the adolescent protagonist—begins his story in this way:

> If you really want to hear about it, the first thing you'll probably want to know is where I was born, and what my lousy childhood was like, and how my parents were occupied and all before they had me, and all that David Copperfield kind of crap, but I don't feel like going into it, if you want to know the truth.

This is a kid with a raw, powerful voice. He's tough and resentful and thinks he's smart enough to know what the reader really wants. He's also filled with a sad and naked anger as he rails against the world. In other words, a hero anybody can relate to.

Because of its voice and its perfect-pitch portrait of a disaffected American teen, this book is as relevant today as it was when it was first published almost sixty years ago. Furthermore, the book continues to sell at racehorse pace.

### 4. Pose a Question

When written skillfully, creating implicit questions is a technique guaranteed to hook a reader. In *Ellen Foster*—a novel whose audience expanded from adults to teens—Kay Gibbons opens her story with these chilling lines:

> When I was little I would think of ways to kill my daddy. I would figure out this or that way and run it down through my head until it got easy.
>
> The way I liked best was letting go a poisonous spider in his bed.

There are plenty of questions to explore here. Why does this girl want to kill her father? What has he done—what was horrible enough—to make her want to kill him in such a hideous way? And, finally, does the girl succeed in killing her father? These questions create a powerful engine that drives the book and carries the reader along for the ride.

## 5. Hint at the Conflict to Come

Conflict is story. Conflict can either be comical or dramatic, scary or tragic. If a character doesn't confront and cope with conflict, he or she can't grow, can't change. Without this transformation, the character is a bore and the plot is thin.

David Baldacci's opening to *Simple Genius* is as riveting as it is mysterious. It also contains portents of the conflict to come:

> There are four acknowledged ways of meeting your maker: You can die by natural causes including illness; you can die by accident; you can die by another's hand; and you can die from your own hand. However, if you live in Washington D.C., there is a fifth way of kicking the bucket: the political death. It can spring from many sources: frolicking in a public fountain with an exotic dancer who is not your wife; stuffing bags of money in your pants when the payer unfortunately happens to be the FBI; or covering up a bungled burglary when you call 1600 Pennsylvania Avenue your home.
>
> Michelle Maxwell was currently stalking the pavement in the nation's capital, but because she wasn't a politician, that fifth choice of mortal exit was not available to her. In fact, the lady was focused only on getting so wasted she'd wake up the next morning with a chunk of her memory gone. There was much she wanted to forget; much that she had to forget.

Who is Michelle Maxwell? Why is she in danger and what kind of danger is she in? Who is she up against? What does she want to forget? All of these urgent questions are posed with a sly smile right at the opening. Future conflict is inevitable, and the question of when, why, and if she will die makes us want to continue reading.

Note the similarity here with Turow's opening. Both authors begin with a list that yanks the reader into the story.

They also write with an edge of humor, posing a question in the reader's head about what sets these two sinners apart from their fellow desperados.

## 6. Anchor the Story in Time and Space

Some readers like to know from the beginning where the story takes place. They appreciate the security of not having to figure out the details—both physical and emotional—surrounding the story.

Consider Danielle Steel's opening for *The Ghost*:

> In the driving rain of a November day, the cab from London to Heathrow took forever. It was so dark it looked like late afternoon, and Charlie Waterston could barely see out the windows as familiar landmarks slid past him. It was only ten o'clock in the morning. And as he leaned his head back against the seat and closed his eyes, he felt as bleak as the weather all around him.
>
> It was hard to believe it had all come to an end. Ten years in London gone, finished, closed, and suddenly behind him. Even now, it was difficult to believe any of it had happened. It had all been so perfect when it began. It had been the start of a life, a career, a decade of excitement and happiness for him in London. And now suddenly, at forty-two, he felt as though all the good times were over. ... Going back to the States. After ten years in London. Nine of them with Carole. Gone now. All of it. In a matter of moments.

What do we know about Charlie besides the fact that he's a candidate for Zoloft? The man is leaving London and his bleak mood matches the November weather. He's stuck in a cab, on his way back to America, and stunned at how he got there.

This opening anchors the reader so she can then travel with Charlie across the Atlantic and learn all about what brought him to this place—and, of course, how he finds new love in the process.

## 7. Generate Anticipation With a Memorable Mood

Daphne du Maurier nails this one perfectly in her gothic tale *Rebecca*. From the first page, the author infuses the story with an ineffable sense of mystery and romance:

> Last night I dreamt I went to Manderley again. It seemed to me I stood by the iron gate leading to the drive, and for a while I could not enter, for the way was barred to me. There was a padlock and chain upon the gate. I called in my dream to the lodge-keeper, and had no answer, and peering closer through the rusted spokes of the gate I saw that the lodge was uninhabited.
>
> No smoke came from the chimney, and the little lattice windows gaped forlorn. Then, like all dreamers, I was possessed of a sudden with supernatural powers and passed like a spirit through the barrier before me. The drive wound away in front of me, twisting and turning as it had always done, but as I advanced I was aware that a change had come upon it; it was narrow and unkept, not the drive that we had known. At first I was puzzled and did not understand, and it was only when I bent my head to avoid the low swinging branch of a tree that I realized what had happened. Nature had come into her own again and, little by little, in her stealthy, insidious way had encroached upon the drive with long tenacious fingers.

Here, mood is everything. A sense of foreboding pervades every word of this opening. Even though the narrator is writing about a dream, it is a dream that hints of a house heavy with secrets ... a house whose appearance matches its past.

## 8. Shock the Reader Into Turning the Page

Hunter S. Thompson pulled off this feat brilliantly in *Fear and Loathing in Las Vegas*. Here's the opening scene:

> We were somewhere around Barstow on the edge of the desert when the drugs began to take hold. I

remember saying something like "I feel a bit lightheaded; maybe you should drive ...." And suddenly there was a terrible roar all around us and the sky was full of what looked like huge bats, all swooping and screeching and diving around the car, which was going about a hundred miles an hour with the top down to Las Vegas. And a voice was screaming: "Holy Jesus! What are these goddamn animals?"

Then it was quiet again. My attorney had taken his shirt off and was pouring beer on his chest, to facilitate the tanning process. "What the hell are you yelling about?" he muttered, staring up at the sun with his eyes closed and covered with wraparound Spanish sunglasses.

"Never mind," I said. "It's your turn to drive."

I hit the brakes and aimed the Great Red Shark toward the shoulder of the highway. No point mentioning those bats, I thought. The poor bastard will see them soon enough.

Outrage meets humor meets disaster. At the very least, you want to turn the page to see if lawyer and client make it to Vegas. At the most, you catch the pile-driver rhythm the author employs and ride the bumpy rails to the end of the book. Either way, it's an effective and unforgettable opening.

In the first chapter of *Shantaram*—a stunning and sprawling novel by Gregory David Roberts—the author creates an opening that encompasses all of these points. At the same time, he offers a profound observation about the human condition.

It took me a long time and most of the world to learn what I know about love and fate and the choices we make, but the heart of it came to me in an instant, while I was chained to a wall and being tortured. I realised, somehow, through the screaming in my mind, that even in that shackled, bloody helplessness, I was still free: free to hate the men who were torturing me, or to forgive them. It doesn't sound like much, I know. But in the flinch and

> bite of the chain, when it's all you've got, that freedom is a universe of possibility. And the choice you make, between hating and forgiving, can become the story of your life.

Here, the author captures your attention in a number of ways. He mixes violence with philosophy. At the same time, he implies that the book is a thriller and a character study. He forces you to question what he did to be tortured, and he definitely reveals a problem. He also creates a mood that is shocking, wise, and introspective. All this is accomplished in 123 words.

## PAY ATTENTION TO OTHER BEGINNINGS

Consider the openings from the following books and ask yourself why they work. Do you want to keep on reading? What makes them compelling? What draws you into the story?

*Middlesex* by Jeffrey Eugenides:

> I was born twice: first, as a baby girl, on a remarkably smogless Detroit day in January of 1960; and then again, as a teenage boy, in an emergency room near Petoskey, Michigan, in August of 1974.

*After* by Robert Anderson:

> For months I had awakened hoping that Fran had died quietly during the night. Quietly. I was terrified of her dying in the agony of cancer. For five years I had been terrified of her pain, or rather, of my having to confront her pain, helplessly.

*The Milagro Beanfield War* by John Nichols:

> Many people in the Miracle Valley had theories about why Joe Mondragón did it.

*The World According to Garp* by John Irving:

> Garp's mother, Jenny Fields, was arrested in Boston in 1942 for wounding a man in a movie theater.

## A WORKING EXAMPLE

Here's my entry into the opening sweepstakes—an example I'll carry on as we examine various writing techniques in the next chapter. Keep in mind that this is merely *one* example of *one* way to open the story. There are as many ways to craft a beginning as there are writers to write it.

> As Jake waited on the platform of the train station, he wondered what the man would look like. They'd never met. And his mother refused to talk about him. All Jake knew was that his father had called him on his twenty-first birthday and said he had something important to give him. Not that Jake gave a damn. He'd lived this long without a father and saw no reason to change that now.
>
> In the distance, the train whistled long and low. What once was familiar and comforting turned into a sad and lonely sound. Jake was tempted to leave. Just walk away from the one-room North Dakota train station and disappear into the searing August heat. He doubted his father would care. The man had twenty-one years to do that. And Jake had never heard one word from him until six days ago.

Here, I tried to give the reader a sense of who the hero is (young, angry, curious, nervous, hopeful, defensive) and at the same time convey what the future might hold for him (conflict, obstacles and resentments, and the possibility of explanation, reconciliation, and forgiveness). There's also the mystery of why Jake's mom refuses to talk about his father and the curiosity about the important "something" his father is bringing him.

All of this is hinted at or spelled out in two short paragraphs. The opening offers several possibilities to me, as an author, depending on which path I choose to take. I don't need to follow every one of those leads; I have options. And I also have room for surprise.

## YOUR BEGINNING

Now that you've read the openings of other books, it's time to create a beginning for your own story. Consider the eight different approaches to grabbing the reader's attention with the opening. Don't be afraid to venture into uncharted territory. Reach outside of your usual writing methods. Then place the hero of your own story in an immediate dilemma.

Include as many of the following elements that you can:

- Present or imply the conflict the hero must face.

- Hint at the reason why this problem is difficult to solve.

- State, or at least suggest, what the hero intends to do about it.

- Anchor the beginning in time and space.

- Write as economically as possible.

Experiment—push your boundaries. Don't settle for the first try. Explore several options. Place your hero somewhere new, either physically or psychologically. Then take a deep breath, give your imagination full rein, and let it run.

# 6

# THE SPACE-TIME CONTINUUM

## Moving Forward (and Backward) Through Your Story

---

*The difference between truth and fiction
is that fiction has to make sense.*

—Mark Twain

Now comes the hard part. You've written an intriguing opening paragraph or two, you've engaged the reader, but what next? One way or the other, you've got to propel the action forward by moving the inciting incident to center stage. Your job now is to yank the reader into the story, then hold her hand so tight—entangle her so skillfully in the action and the lives of the characters—that she won't want to let go.

How do you accomplish this goal? You analyze your opening and tell the story that evolves out of it.

# THREE APPROACHES TO STORYTELLING

Let's return to the opening about Jake that I began in chapter five. There are three basic ways to handle the rest of that story: the Forward March, the Total Flashback, or the Zigzag method. As you might guess, however, there's wiggle room within each of the conventions that allows you to create your own variations on these basic themes.

## I. Forward March

The first way to approach the continuation of the story is to move forward in time in a linear fashion. Go from A to B to C to D to E. No stopping, no doubling back. The plot moves in strict chronological order.

### *Advantages of Forward March*

- It is easier to devise and organize a plot in this way.

- Moving the story ahead in a linear fashion is less fraught with literary traps and convoluted plot devices.

- It is a simpler technique to master.

### *Disadvantages of Forward March*

- It's difficult to tell a complete and textured story without shifting back and forth in time.

- Without the use of flashbacks—a technique in which you interject a scene or scenes that happened prior to the current action—your storytelling options are limited.

When I wrote my first novel, I'd never taken a writing class. As a consequence, I wasn't consciously aware of techniques that authors use to create a story. All I knew was that I was an enthusiastic reader and a good writer and I had a story I wanted to tell. The problem was, I didn't know how to go about telling it.

One of the first challenges I encountered was how to move from one point in time to another. After writing the first ten pages of the book, I came to a screeching halt when I realized I didn't know how to make a transition in time or space. A practical consequence of this lack of basic knowledge was that I couldn't move from one scene to the next.

An author friend of mine, David Markson, read my opening pages and paid me a high compliment: He told me I could write. When I explained I didn't know how to move forward in time, he suggested I solve the challenge of structuring the plot by writing the book in strict chronological order. Grateful for his encouragement of my naive efforts, I took his suggestion. As a matter of fact, I applied a literal interpretation to his advice, allotting one chapter for each day of the week. The novel begins on a Sunday and finishes on a Saturday. Furthermore, each chapter opens in the morning and closes at night. No skipping, no doubling back. Structure 101.

With that concept in mind, let's return to Jake at the train station and see how this story might play out in a straightforward, chronological way.

> ... In the distance, the train whistled long and low. What once was a familiar and comforting sound turned into a lonely wail. Jake was tempted to leave. Just walk away from the one-room train station and disappear into the hot August day. He doubted his father would care.
>
> Standing there, he'd never felt more alone in his life. As the train rounded the brown dusty hill in the distance, Jake's heart beat faster and his breathing took on the rhythm of the engine. Chuga chuga, chuga chuga.
>
> He held his back straight, his hands at his side. The knuckles turned white on his clenched fists.
>
> *Chuga ... Chuga ... Chuga ... Sssssssssssss*
>
> Oh God, Jake thought, please don't let him be an asshole. Let him at least have a good excuse. His stomach twisted into an impossible knot as he saw a man—dark, brush-cut hair, black eyes, and a nervous expression on his face—step onto the platform and

look around. He carried a small suitcase and a package
the size of a shoebox wrapped in brown paper.

"Jake?" he said.

Jake nodded. Then he stepped forward to meet the
stranger who was his father.

It's possible to end the opening right here, either with a chapter
break or a double space. That way, we leave the scene with plenty
of unanswered questions, the primary ones being the need to
know what's in the package and what's the man's excuse for
twenty-one years of neglect.

In the next section, we could pick up on father and son
walking away from the station. The story is then told in linear
fashion—a straight journey forward into the future as one
scene unfolds into the next. From the initial meeting at the
train station, we move through Jake's first awkward moments
with his dad. Then the two men walk to the motel where the
father checks in before he takes Jake to lunch at the local café.
During this time, he never lets the mysterious package leave
his side.

We continue through the story as Jake tries to resist falling under the spell of this charismatic man. Maybe his mom
won't talk about him because she never stopped loving him,
Jake thinks ... or is that wishful thinking? At the same time
that he's entertaining possibilities, Jake struggles with the push-
pull feelings directed at a father who abandoned him before he
was born.

As the story unfolds, we watch as Jake gradually comes
to understand that his wish for his parents' reconciliation is
doomed to failure. And in the process, we witness how painful
the eventual meeting is for his mother.

In this straightforward approach to telling the tale, we
move in chronological order through the story—from A to
Z without any flashbacks, without any movement back and
forth in time. The momentum is always toward the future,
toward wanting to know what happens next, never toward
the past.

## 2. Total Flashback

The Total Flashback is used when you want to shift from the present action of the story into the past. Then you tell the story from that perspective as you move toward the present again. You might do this because you want to:

- Clue the reader in on a secret about the hero's earlier life.

- Offer background information about a plot element.

- Give the reader information about the subplot.

- Contribute to the development of a subplot.

- Enlighten the reader about an aspect of a character.

- Add texture and complexity to a character and his life.

- Explore and explain why the character is the way he is.

Using this technique, you could open the story with the section that takes place in the train station, present time. Then you shift back to an earlier point in time. When you move into the past, you tell the backstory of the hero, working your way up to the present again—that moment when Jake meets his father. You come full circle and then move forward. As you complete the backstory, you have a full range of plot possibilities to explore before you reach the end of the book.

### Advantages of Total Flashback

- It opens up the story to the past and allows you to include information that would be absent in the strict chronological telling of a tale.

- You can add critical backstory information that lends texture and depth to your narrative.

- With the exception of the initial flashback, you still have the simplicity of dealing with a fundamentally forward-moving plot.

## Disadvantages of Total Flashback

- Unless this approach is executed with skill, the reader could get confused about what's then and what's now.

- It is a more demanding technique to master.

In the Total Flashback method, we begin at the point where the father steps off the train. Then we move back in time and live through Jake's attempts to find his father, watching as he encounters one obstacle after another.

> ... Jake's breath caught in his throat as the train pulled to a stop. Oh God, he thought, please don't be an asshole. Don't let me hate my father. And don't let him bring me something awful that I'm stuck with for the rest of my life.
>
> The young man stood paralyzed, trying to fathom why he had chosen to meet this man. He and his mom had a good life. They loved each other and had gotten along just fine without a husband and father.
>
> Not that life had been easy. But he'd just graduated from college. He had good friends and he had Duke—a black mutt with a tan snout and eyebrows, and a white stripe on his nose.
>
> Jake's mom gave him the puppy around the time he started to ask persistent questions about his father. He was fourteen years old, getting ready to begin high school.
>
> "Why don't you ever talk about my father?" Jake had asked at Thanksgiving dinner. Family time. Grandpa cleared his throat and looked down at his plate. His grandmother picked up a platter and carried it to the kitchen.
>
> Susan Davidson reached across the table and took her son's hand. A soft sigh escaped her lips.
>
> "Your dad left before you were born," she'd said. Her voice was quiet, showing little emotion. "I don't know where he is."
>
> "What's his name?"

"Nathan. Nathan Sinclair."

"Someday I will meet that man and ask him why he left me," Jake said.

You've got the idea. We've shifted the story back in time to when Jake was fourteen years old. We then follow his life as he begins the search for his father.

In this approach, you've set the hook in the reader's mind by posing unspoken questions. Is the father dead or alive? Did Jake search for his father? Did he locate him and decide not to see him? How did his father make contact? Does Jake have half-siblings that he doesn't know about?

By moving back in time like this, you create certain expectations in the reader. And it is your obligation to meet every one of them. The fact is, when you use Total Flashback, you make implicit promises to the reader that certain information will be revealed, and that certain scenes will play out. In this case, you must eventually offer answers all those unspoken questions posed in the opening.

## Techniques for Total Flashback

**Create a powerful opening scene.** In Total Flashback, it's critical that you set up an opening scene powerful and memorable enough for the reader to want to return to it. This not only provides a strong anchor for the reader—one that keeps the storyline steady and marks the point of return—it also grabs the reader's interest enough to keep reading.

If you just have Jake going to the train station and waiting for someone, that wouldn't make me want to continue reading long enough to find out who he's meeting or what he's doing there. You need to pose questions the reader will want to have answered—questions provocative enough for her to stick around in order to have her curiosity satisfied. Here are the questions I planted as I wrote that opening scene:

- What happened between Jake's mom and dad?

- What if Jake and his dad don't get along?

- Why hasn't the father contacted his son after all these years?

- What is this special thing the father wants to give his son?

**Anchor the story.** When dealing with a Total Flashback, it's important to be clear about when the flashback takes place in relation to the opening scene so the reader is properly oriented in the story. Otherwise, you create book-closing frustration instead of page-turning suspense.

What have we learned in the opening paragraphs of my example that anchors the scene in the reader's mind?

- Jake is twenty-one years old when he goes to the train station. He's alone and he's scared as he waits to meet this stranger who happens to be his father.

- A connection is made between his new puppy and his first serious questions about his father, as we flash back to when Jake was fourteen years old. This informs the reader that there is a seven-year period of time that must be spanned in order to return to the present—creating a time frame to orient the reader, informing her where she's come from and where she is going.

These elements not only intrigue the reader, they create expectations. Like keeping a promise, the observation of the rituals that inform the reader and resolve the story are not optional. If you keep all your promises to the reader, the reader will honor you by sticking with your story until the end.

**Play catch-up.** Even though you've gone back in time, the reader naturally assumes you will move forward until you finally arrive at the train station again. That's the contract you set up when you move into a flashback. And it is a contract you break at the risk of angering the reader.

**Dramatize critical scenes.** Another aspect of your contract with the reader is that you will dramatize the meeting with the father in full. That's the implicit promise you made in the opening paragraphs. You cannot, must not, have Jake meet his dad "offstage," that is, refer to the meeting without ever dramatizing it in present time. Nor can you have Jake meet his dad on the last page of the story and leave the reader hanging. That's playing dirty pool with the reader.

Readers want to know what happened, why it happened, and how it turned out. When you don't play out the big dramatic moment that they've been anticipating throughout the book, the reading experience becomes anticlimactic.

**Calculate timing.** Plan to return to the present (in this case, have Jake and his father come together at the station again) about two-thirds of the way through the book. This gives you ample opportunity to carry through with the story in present time, to find out what's in the package, and to wrap up the plot about Jake and his father. You also have time to play out the subplots of his mother's fear of losing her son to this interloper and the mending of her strained relationship with the man she once loved.

## 3. Zigzag

The flashback has a long and venerable history as a storytelling device. You can use it in one grand, full-circle sweep, as in the Total Flashback.

Or you can write the story in a forward timeline until you reach a moment where you need to fill in some detail from the past or add a particularly suspenseful or memorable scene. Then you slip into a mini-flashback before returning to the present-time story.

### Advantages of Zigzag

- It allows considerable flexibility in how you tell the story and what you allow your reader to know.

- You can provide needed background material whenever you want to include it.

- You can use it to pique the curiosity of the reader or increase suspense.

- You can create layered characters and plot complications.

- It allows you to weave in critical information as you move forward with the plot.

## Disadvantages of Zigzag

- Unless this approach is used with skill, the reader can get confused between past and present.

- It is the most challenging technique to master.

Let's return to the railroad station one more time and play the scene the zigzag way:

> ... Jake stood silent and alone, remembering the times he was teased about not having a father, and how he beat the crap out of Eddie Sanchez for taunting him.
>
> Now, on this hot August day, Jake wondered why he'd bothered to come to the station. As the train rounded the brown, dusty hill in the distance and bore down on him, his heart beat faster and his breathing took on the rhythm of the engine. *Chuga chuga, chuga chuga. Chuga ... Chuga ... Chuga ... Ssssssssssss*
>
> His back straight and his hands at his side, Jake felt paralyzed as the train pulled to a stop. For the life of him, he couldn't figure out why he had agreed to meet this man—this stranger.
>
> I must be crazy, he thought. Why did I ever decide to mess with it? And on top of all that, Mom is in total meltdown over the meeting.
>
> "Are you sure you know what you're doing?" she'd asked when Jake told her he had contacted his father. They'd been gathering eggs when he broke the news.
>
> "Of course I know," Jake had said.
>
> "I hope you're right," his mom said. Her hand shook as she set a speckled brown egg in the basket she carried.
>
> Now, all alone, Jake wasn't so sure he'd done the right thing. He wondered if his e-mail agreement to meet his father would change his life forever. He wasn't so sure he could deal with that. Or if he wanted to.

Jake liked life on the farm. And now, armed with his degree in agricultural science, he was confident he'd make a good farmer. Besides, it was time for this land to be put to good use. Like George Washington and Thomas Jefferson before him, industrial hemp would be his crop.

The farm suited him. He was close enough to town to see his friends and far enough away to have the freedom of the wide open spaces. For as long as he could remember, Jake had owned his own horse. First it was just an old nag named Silver Lady. Then, for his sixteenth birthday, his grandpa had given him a sorrel quarter horse.

He also had a dog named Duke. Man and dog went everywhere together. It was hard to leave Duke home on this particular day. But Jake didn't want anything to distract him from his mission. Besides, Duke was scared of trains.

Jake watched the engine as it pulled to a stop at the station. Or what passed as a station in Shiloh, North Dakota, population 2,372.

His breath caught in his throat. Oh God, he thought, please don't let me hate him. His stomach twisted into an impossible knot as a man stepped onto the platform and looked around.

"Jake?" he said.

Jake nodded and stepped forward to meet the stranger who was his father.

As you can see, this method is something of a dance—a minuet in which you touch and let go. Return to your corner to provide a spot of background, then you move forward to continue the dance. One step forward, one step back; five steps forward, two steps back. If this is done skillfully, the reader isn't even aware of the different movements in time. You're simply filling in details as you come to them.

Occasionally, you might include a longer flashback. When you do, always make certain it is clear where you are when you return to the present time. Otherwise, you run the risk of confusing the reader.

## CHOOSING THE WAY

In this chapter, I've shown you one story and three ways to tell it. Now try it on your story. Write your opening again, experimenting with the three different ways to tell your story. When choosing one of the flashback techniques, consider the following:

- Which method makes you feel the most comfortable?
- Which technique is the best fit for the story you want to tell?
- What is the strongest way to tell the story?

Once you've found the technique that suits you best, ask yourself the following questions:

- Did I present my contract clearly?
- Did I pose interesting questions?
- Have I created a compelling conflict?
- Have I uncovered an interesting problem?
- Have I presented an interesting character?
- Have I given the reader a hero to root for?
- Have I built an intriguing foundation?
- Have I kept all my promises?

## THE INHERENT SENSE OF STORY

In fiction, every event demands a cause, and every cause demands an effect. If you plant a seed, it must sprout. Furthermore, you must plant the seed in front of the reader before you show her the sprout. These are the rules. I hasten to add that Charles

Dickens and his ilk, who traffic successfully in coincidence and surprise, take exception to those rules. But we mere storytelling mortals are doomed to follow the law. Otherwise, we lose credibility with our reader.

It's natural to feel overwhelmed by the multiple challenges of storytelling. You've just tossed these introductory balls in the air. Now what? How do you juggle all those plot points without dropping them in a heap of loose story threads and a tangled plot?

It's the writer's task to gather together the disparate elements of plot and character and to integrate them into a cohesive whole. Boiled down to its essence, storytelling is no more than the imposition of order on imagined experience. Making sense of the events in your story so they make sense to your reader is a critical goal of story. To my mind, the only time you can get away with a genuine, random event is at the opening of the book. Something happens. Something unanticipated. Something unusual. Something fabulous or puzzling or horrific. This event—the inciting incident—then sets off a chain of actions and reactions that comprise the middle of your story and lead to the inevitable end.

Whether you tell this story in chronological order, in flashback, or in mini-flashbacks, the rest of your book grows out of those opening events.

## 7

# ENTER THE BITCH
## The Power of Negative Voices

*It's easy, after all, not to be a writer. Most people aren't writers, and very little harm comes to them.*

—Julian Barnes

About this time, you're feeling happy as a toad full of flies. You've crafted a dynamite opening that will hook any reader with an I.Q. above room temperature. You've conjured up the beginning of a fabulous story filled with intriguing characters, and you're making a beeline toward a Pulitzer or an Oscar.

Then you reach the beginning of the *middle* of your story. That's when your most destructive internal critic steps out of the wings and onto the stage of your consciousness. With her mouth pursed and her arms crossed, a nasty smile flickers across her lips. The Bitch has been waiting for this moment.

"Everybody knows you're a fake," she whispers with a squint-eyed smirk. "What *ever* made you think you could write a book?"

Stunned, you step back. That's when she moves in for the kill. "You got yourself into this mess." Significant pause. "*Now* let's see you get out of it!"

For the record: We've all got Bitches. Men have them. Women have them. This is not a gender-specific role. My Bitch happens to be female and speaks in a soft whisper. But if your petty tyrant has a voice that makes pronouncements in a *basso profundo* and belongs to a man who shaves three times a day, feel free to call him The Son of The Bitch.

Whatever the gender of your beast, instead of cowering, take a deep breath and tell that double-dealing, undermining, life-negating, confidence-stealing dominatrix to shut her mouth, back off your personal stage, and stay in the basement where she belongs.

## INNER VOICE, NOT INNER TRUTH

I have just given you great advice. Remember it. Cherish it. Place it at the front of your creative shelf so you can stroke it every day. In the interest of truth, however, I'm forced to confess that this gem of wisdom—this life-polished pearl of perspicacity—falls into that familiar but slippery category labeled Easier Said Than Done.

The reason our internal voice has gotten away with its negative nonsense for so long is that we haven't paid attention to it ... at least consciously. This Darth Vader of the psyche has probably been whispering in your ear all your life. In fact, most of our toxic tapes run on a continuous loop.

We become so accustomed to hearing the venomous voices, we don't even register them with our conscious minds. That doesn't mean, however, our unconscious mind isn't picking up on the content. So our task as a writer—and as a human being—is to become aware of these voices in order to mute their impact and to allow us to live the full creative life we deserve.

Alas, accomplishing this task isn't always easy. As British writer and journalist Paul Johnson once said, "It cannot be emphasized too strongly that balanced, well-adjusted, stable, and secure people do not, on the whole, make good writers, including good journalists."

With that insight in mind, I can personally attest to the fact that becoming aware of—as well as transforming—our negative internal messages is one of life's greatest challenges. I've put my shrink's two kids through college in my efforts to quell my own voices that—to date—have proven they know how to manifest defeat in 731 ways.

Given that I've had more than a tad of experience in this field of study, I can offer you some hard-won advice.

## Thoughts From a Wounded Veteran of the Self-Confidence Wars

- Trust me: If you don't face The Bitch now, she'll taunt you for the rest of your book. Or more likely for the rest of your life. And she'll do her best to convince you to give up writing while you can still find regular, reliable, long-term employment that occupies you both day *and* night.

- Confronting the voices is like quitting smoking. There's never a good time to do it. Ergo: Do it now.

- Just because a voice speaks to you from within does not mean it speaks the truth.

- Negative voices run on automatic pilot and depend on you to do the same. That's how they've become such an integral part of your mental wallpaper and assumed so much power.

- The way to mute the intensity of the message is to become aware of the voices and how they undermine your confidence.

## CHOOSE CREATIVITY: HOME REMEDIES

As you lie in bed and do your deep belly breathing, open yourself to the thoughts that drift past you in wispy, barely heard whispers. The ones that say things like:

"Psst! Give up now before you embarrass yourself."

"What ever made you think you could actually write a novel?"

"You never were any good at finishing a task."

"You're not (choose three of the following adjectives): *smart, skilled, talented, creative, deserving, clever, wise, imaginative, productive, disciplined, capable, qualified, educated, experienced, gifted, inventive, realistic, interesting* enough to pull this book off."

Who are these negative thoughts coming from? A critical parent? A former teacher? A boss? Identifying the speakers isn't always possible. But if you can put a face to the voice, it helps remove the sting from the words.

When you hear the voices, learn to identify the feelings that accompany them. Once you've got a handle on what the feelings are, allow yourself to experience them fully—both physically and emotionally—then let them go. (This is another one of those Easier Said Than Done situations. Nevertheless, with will and intent set firmly in place, it is possible to accomplish this feat.)

Every time you hear the voice, acknowledge its presence but not its power. Remind yourself that this is a voice, not a reality. It no longer speaks to you with authority. Sometimes you'll only catch a phrase or a few well-chosen words. (*You're only ... You'll never ... You can't ... I can't believe you did such a stupid ...*)

But if you listen carefully as you go about your daily tasks—if you practice awareness—you'll realize that the voices are running in the back of your mind all day long. They're accustomed to being able to speak undisturbed. The mere fact that you bring the voices into your awareness is enough to diminish some of their power.

Once you've become aware of the messages, you can begin to replace them with more positive words. (*Creativity is my birthright. This is a terrific idea for a story and I am the one to write it. Just because I've never written a book or screenplay before doesn't mean I can't write one now. I am wise enough to know what I don't know. I am smart enough to learn what I don't know. And I am talented enough to write what I do know.*) Think *The Little Engine That Could.*

## TRICKS OF THE TRADE
### Once Is Not Enough

In order to keep The Bitch or The Son of The Bitch in check, you must make awareness a lifelong habit. This is a reasonable price to pay for creative freedom.

## REALITY CHECK

You can't get rid of the voices; you can't just spray Raid over the dark corners of your psyche, poison the creepy-crawly negativity, and be done with it. But you can make room for the voices so they no longer have the capacity to wreak havoc on your confidence. By making awareness a part of your daily life, you diminish the power of the voices and expand the parameters and possibilities of your creative life.

# 8

# THE MID-STORY CRISIS

## Rescuing Your Story
## From the Middle Muddle

---

*Thirty years ago my older brother, who was ten
years old at the time, was trying to get a report
on birds written that he'd had three months to
write ... He was at the kitchen table close to
tears ... immobilized by the hugeness of the task
ahead. Then my father sat down beside him, put
his arm around my brother's shoulder, and said,
"Bird by bird, buddy. Just take it bird by bird."*

—Anne Lamott

Women go through menopause and get hot flashes. Men suffer a
midlife crisis and buy a Porsche. Writers hit the middle muddle
and freeze. This is nothing new. In 1320, Dante Alighieri wrote
about the entry into the Inferno in *The Divine Comedy,* illumi-
nating the challenges inherent in middles: "In the middle of the

journey of life, I came to myself within a dark wood where the straight way was lost. Ah, how hard it is to tell of that wood, savage and harsh and dense, the thought of which renews my fear. So bitter is it that death is hardly more."

Even though Dante is talking about life and we're talking about fiction, they might as well be one and the same.

## WHAT NEXT?

So here's the situation: You've just written a terrific opening. You've created a razzle-dazzle, whoop-de-doo, bang-up beginning to your story. And you've accomplished all the goals you set for yourself: You have hinted at conflict, posed intriguing questions, presented a problem, created great characters, and hooked the reader. At this point you might be tempted to ask, "Where do I go from here? How do I peel the layers of the fabulous fictional onion I just had the temerity to create?"

Trust me on this point: If you're anxious about what to do next, you are not alone. There are few writers who have moved past the opening of their books without wondering how to proceed.

The answer to this dilemma is simple and straightforward: What you do next grows out of what you've already done. One thing leads to another that leads to another. To borrow from Robert Frost, you've got promises to keep.

## THE THROUGHLINE AS LIFELINE

So now you've reached into the heart of the book, that painful place where—like Hansel and Gretel—it's not uncommon to become lost in the dark, savage wood. It's scary in there. Intimidating. Confusing. The Bitch or The Son of The Bitch is lurking behind every tree, waiting to grab you as you struggle to move forward. It's easy to become frightened and lose your way. But as someone once said to me when I was tangled in the midst of a serious personal crisis, "The only way out is *through*, Nancy. The only way out is through." This bit of wisdom applies to fiction as well as life.

The best way to travel the length of your story is to grab hold of the throughline—the driving force of the book that you set up in the opening pages—and refuse to let go. There can, of course, be more than one throughline in a story. But as you will see, there should always be one fundamental throughline that pulls the reader from beginning to end.

## TRICKS OF THE TRADE
### Do It Now

Before the end of the first chapter, make an effort to set up the primary throughline of your book. By creating a natural trajectory for your story's development, the plot will unfold in a more organic way and you'll feel more comfortable in moving forward. This is also insurance against getting sidetracked. You can set up your through-line in an outline, or you can wing it. Either way, make the effort to establish this critical introductory plot point from the beginning.

In Hollywood, screenwriters speak of the throughline as an unwavering given in a screenplay. They also refer to it as the spine of the story. The throughline is the central plot point that propels the hero from beginning to end—from one scene to the next, from one act to the next. The throughline creates the forward momentum that makes the story absorbing and the protagonist spring to life.

Some screenwriters think of throughline as the embodiment of the main character's conscious desire. The character knows what he wants and knows that he wants it. This personal hunger, shared by the viewer, drives the story and shapes the narrative.

Somewhere at the closing of the second act of a screenplay—or the end of the middle of a book—the character's conscious desire breaks down. What he wants is denied him, either by choice or by the force of outside circumstances. This breakdown then exposes a deeper motivation—a motivation he was originally unaware of—that propels the character forward.

This thirst—this force that motivates the hero and drives the action—becomes a secondary, but equally powerful, throughline.

Just as a screenwriter constructs a throughline for his story, an actor constructs a throughline for his role in a play or movie. As he moves through the play, he thinks of the throughline as his objective, a guiding light he follows from beginning to end. Whatever the situation in which he finds himself, he does not lose sight of this goal, this throughline.

The actor also has an objective for each scene—a mini-throughline, a driving motivation that guides him from the beginning to the end of the scene. It might be as simple as wanting to make a polite exit from a room when another character won't stop talking, or as complicated as trying to divert a character's attention from the dead body in the closet. Either way, the throughline is there to keep the actor on track—which is precisely what it does for a writer.

## The Guiding (Green) Light

In *The Great Gatsby*, F. Scott Fitzgerald focuses the story on Jay Gatsby and his abiding love for Daisy Buchanan. The story is narrated by Daisy's cousin Nick Carraway, who bears witness to—and participates in—the tragedy that unfolds before him.

Jay Gatsby was born into poverty. But as a young military officer in WWI Louisville, he meets and falls hopelessly in love with Daisy, a woman who later marries another man for his status and money, instead of for love.

After the war, Gatsby makes a fortune during prohibition by smuggling alcohol and trading illegal securities. His only aim is to earn enough money to court Daisy again on her own turf—which encompasses upper-class wealth and all the trappings that go with it. Everything Gatsby does, every decision he makes, is propelled by his love for Daisy and his need to prove himself worthy of her attention. It doesn't matter to him that she is a married woman. She is all he wants in life.

Even though he hasn't seen Daisy since he left for the war, Gatsby buys a house near the Long Island mansion where she lives with her husband, Tom Buchanan. He then proceeds to accumulate all the status symbols of wealth—from fine clothes to rare antiques—that he thinks will help him win Daisy's affection. He also throws one lavish party after another in the hope that Daisy will somehow appear.

One day after Nick moves into a small house next door to Gatsby's mansion, a formal invitation to one of Gatsby's parties is delivered by the butler. Intrigued, Nick attends the gala. What he doesn't yet understand is that his neighbor has been throwing parties for five years, all in the hope of finding someone who could introduce him to Daisy Buchanan again.

Midway through the story, a friend of Nick's tells him that Gatsby had confessed to her that he bought his estate because it was near the mansion where Daisy lived. It's then that Nick remembers how Gatsby had opened his arms one night to the green light glowing across the water—the green light at the end of Tom and Daisy Buchanan's dock … and the light Gatsby stares at as he dreams of his future with Daisy.

Eventually, Nick is maneuvered into inviting Daisy to tea so that Gatsby can reunite with his old flame. At the reunion, the two fall in love all over again. And as the party shifts to Gatsby's house, they ignore Nick to such an extent that he finally leaves.

Throughout the story of mysteries posed and relationships done and undone, the reader is never allowed to forget Jay Gatsby's one unbending ambition—to win Daisy Buchanan. Blinded by naive romanticism and searing obsession, he is incapable of seeing Daisy's life and values for what they are: ostentatious, shallow, and artificial.

In fact, Gatsby is so driven to win Daisy away from her husband that in the tragic denouement, he's even willing to take the blame for being the driver of the car that runs over and kills Myrtle Wilson—Tom Buchanan's mistress. The truth is that it was Daisy at the wheel of the car. Even though he knows his wife killed Myrtle, Tom allows Myrtle's husband, George, to believe Gatsby was the driver. As a result, the next day George goes to Gatsby's house, then shoots and kills him.

Throughout the book of relationships won and lost, of openings exploited and pasts revealed, Gatsby's relentless pursuit of his elusive dream is the throughline that propels the action from the beginning to the end of this perfectly constructed novel. The irony is that this blind pursuit of his dream is not only the reason for Jay Gatsby's success; it is also the cause of his downfall and death.

## The Speeding Locomotive: Throughline in a Nutshell

Consider *The Little Engine That Could*—a story we've all read and that addresses throughline at its most fundamental level. This classic children's story begins with a train carrying toys and food to the good little boys and girls on the other side of the mountain. The desire to make the delivery is the original and sustaining throughline of the book. The train's got the goods. The children are waiting.

Before the train can make it over the mountain, however, the original engine breaks down, jeopardizing the delivery of toys and food. The dolls on the train ask three engines for help, but they all refuse. Finally the dolls ask a tiny blue engine and, reluctant but willing, he agrees to help.

Here, the throughline shifts from the need to deliver toys to the engine's challenge of pulling the train over the mountain. Will he or won't he be able to accomplish this daunting task? The last third of the story is then propelled by this secondary throughline, moving from *I-think-I-can* to *I-thought-I-could* in a tale that has entertained and encouraged young children for seventy-five years.

Although the focus shifts midway through the story to the new throughline of finding and receiving help—along with the Little Engine's heroic efforts to make it over the mountain—the overarching throughline of the book still remains. Even as we cheer for the success of the Little Engine, we never forget that the boys and girls on the other side of the mountain are waiting for their goodies.

Continuing the train motif, think of the throughline as a locomotive carrying your main character on the journey through your book. With the exception of experimental novels and other avant-garde forms, you move down the track in one direction only. You might stop at stations, take on new passengers and let others off, admire the views, even grab a bite for lunch. But always—no matter what—you maintain a forward-moving trajectory. You never lose sight of your goal. You might change tracks or take a side trip, but you don't bring the throughline to a halt before it connects to the next throughline—or before it reaches the final destination. Even if you employ the liberal use of flashbacks and the multiple subplots, the momentum is always and inevitably moving forward toward your final destination.

From beginning to end, the throughline is the constant in your story. You can have any number of other things happening in the book. But the matter of what drives the hero and compels him to act is never in question because the throughline is there to maintain the reader's attention and to pull him through the story.

## Take a Ride on the Throughline

Take a moment to think about your story strictly in terms of throughline. Then ask yourself the following questions:

- What is the primary throughline of my story?

- What are the secondary throughlines of my story?

- What does my hero want, why can't she have it, and what is the driving force that makes her do anything, endure anything, overcome anything to achieve her goal?

- How do these throughline threads intersect?

- How does each throughline contribute to the forward momentum of the story?

- How does each throughline pull the reader through the story?

If you can't answer these questions with confidence, take the time to think about them and to devise ways you can make the throughlines stronger. Once you've fixed your focus on the throughlines, you can use them to power the plot throughout your story.

# CLASSICAL DRAMA
## In the Age of the Page-Turner

---

*One of the few things I know about writing is this: spend it all, shoot it, play it, lose it, all, right away every time. Do not hoard what seems good for a later place in the book, or for another book; give it, give it all, give it now.*

—Annie Dillard

We've already talked about the inciting incident in classical Greek drama—the original catalyst that creates the opposing forces of action and reaction. Although the structure of classical drama might seem irrelevant when compared to the elements that go into contemporary storytelling, the two are closely related. In fact, this Greek drama stuff isn't as outdated or remote as it first appears. Furthermore, an understanding of the structure will help you in all your storytelling efforts in the future.

## BASIC DRAMATIC STRUCTURE

According to *A Handbook to Literature* by William Flint Thrall and Addison Hibbard, classical dramatic structure is divided into distinct, identifiable parts:

1. Rising action
   a. Exciting force (what we've been referring to as inciting incident)
   b. Conflict and complications

2. Climax

3. Falling action
   a. The reversal
   b. The resolution
   c. The last moment of suspense

Imagine these elements as a triangle with the climax at the peak. When represented visually, scholarly types call this Freytag's Pyramid—named, as I discovered, after German playwright and literary critic Gustav Freytag, who devised a chart similar to the one below in 1863.

Whether the classical Greek dramatist was dealing with comedy or tragedy, these critical story elements did not change. Twenty-five hundred years later, this structure remains both useful and relevant.

Although I trust you're not writing a mother-son drama called *Oedipus Joins the Country Club,* looking at your story from this classical point of view is an effective way to move your action forward to its logical, organic conclusion.

## Everything Old Is New Again

No doubt there are those among you who believe that these classical guidelines are *so* yesterday. Allow me to disabuse you of this notion by parsing two dramas—one ancient and one modern—to demonstrate how aptly the old applies to the new.

The first is *Oedipus Rex,* a complicated and—by any measure—shocking drama crafted by Sophocles around 429 B.C.

**Background:** When the story opens, Oedipus, the king of Thebes, is married to an older woman named Jocasta, whose first husband, King Laius, was murdered. Oedipus had basically won the right to marry the queen by being the only man in the Greek equivalent of *Jeopardy!* who could answer the Riddle of the Sphinx (*What goes on four legs in the morning, on two legs at noon, and on three legs in the evening?*). Being a tad insecure about his jackpot-winning place on the throne, Oedipus suspects that Jocasta's brother Creon has his greedy eye fixed on his kingly position.

**Inciting incident:** When the drama opens, the people of Thebes are plagued by plague. Jocasta's brother Creon has just returned from the Oracle of Apollo where he learned that the plague won't be lifted until the murderer of King Laius is identified and punished for his crime. Oedipus, with more than a touch of hubris, announces he will uncover the cause of the plague. And thus he asks Tiresias, the local seer, for help.

**Conflict and complications:** Tiresias—who suspects why the plague has been visited upon Thebes—suggests in no uncertain terms that the king shouldn't ask and definitely shouldn't tell. Oedipus ignores the seer's warning and chooses to do it his way. In the process, he manages to piss off Tiresias big time when he accuses the prophet of being in cahoots with Jocasta's brother, Creon, so the wannbe king can ascend to the throne.

Further complicating the issue, Jocasta mentions to her husband that it will be hard to find the killer of Laius since he'd been slain by a stranger at a place where three roads meet. This news sets Oedipus's antennae aquiver, since he'd once encountered an angry mob in a similar location and had, in fact, killed a man there. On the other hand, his own father is still alive, so the king doesn't lose that much sleep over the coincidence.

**Climax:** Disregarding the adage (attributed to everyone from Sun Tzu to Machiavelli to Don Corleone) that you should keep your friends close and your enemies closer, Oedipus gets Creon out of the way by sending his brother-in-law into exile. Needless to say, the mistreatment of her brother upsets Jocasta, who then asks the Oracle of Apollo what it has to say about the family feud.

The oracle pronounces that the queen's deceased husband, King Laius, was slain by their own child. But Jocasta scoffs at that news. When she and her husband were newlyweds, they heard a prophesy that the king would be killed by his own son. As a consequence of the prediction, when Jocasta got pregnant and gave birth to a son, they put tough love into practice, bound the newborn infant's legs together, and abandoned him on Mount Cithaero. That being the case, the presumably dead baby couldn't possibly have killed his father.

**Reversal:** A messenger arrives to tell Oedipus that his father, Polybus, has just died. And he had died of natural causes, which the king is relieved to hear. But his relief is short-lived. Because the messenger then breaks the news to Oedipus that Polybus wasn't his real father; that he was actually an abandoned infant who'd been rescued by a shepherd and given to Polybus and his wife to be raised as their own.

More than a little distressed by the possibility that he's committed patricide, the young king visits the Oracle of Apollo where the shocking news is confirmed: Oedipus not only murdered his own father, he is—*gulp*—both father and brother of his mother/wife's children.

**Resolution:** In those days, ignorance was no excuse. Nor was denial. The faster Oedipus fled from his fate as defined by the oracles, the closer he moved towards it. Finally, the king is forced to break the disturbing news to his wife that he is not only her husband ... he is also her son. Understandably freaked by this kink in her family dynamic, Jocasta retires to the palace and hangs herself by her own hair.

**Last moment of suspense:** When Oedipus discovers the death by tress, he's so horrified by the demise of his mother/wife—not to mention the fact that his children/siblings are seriously upset—that he removes the brooch from the queen's gown and pokes out his eyes. At least if he's blind, he'll be unable to witness the results of his own horrific actions.

*Sic transit Oedipus Rex:* Blood dripping from his eyes, Oedipus asks his brother-in-law/uncle Creon (who has returned from exile to assume the throne) if Antigone and Ismene—the sisters he fathered with Jocasta—could stay with him to tend to his needs. Creon refuses. And thus the new king leads Oedipus into exile where he is doomed to wander, blind and tormented, for the remainder of his days ... an ending that embodies the thought expressed by Anonymous when he said, "To achieve tragic proportions, a hero must have a moment of clarity and self-knowledge."

## Déjà Vu All Over Again

To analyze how this same Classical story structure applies to modern fiction, consider *Presumed Innocent,* Scott Turow's thriller that after twenty-two years and eight million copies, is now in its forty-third printing. Although the story doesn't feature incest and prophecies, the author makes up for it in blood, gore, sex, and sheer page-turning thrills.

**Background:** Narrated in first-person present tense, the premise of the book is grounded in the story of Rusty Sabich, Kindle County Deputy Prosecuting Attorney, and his search for justice within the context of "truth." His wife Barbara teaches mathematics at the local university. And they have one son named Nat, whom Rusty adores, partially because the boy symbolizes family wholeness for a man who comes from a tormented background.

**Inciting incident:** Carolyn Polhemus—beautiful, ambitious, and sensual Deputy Prosecuting Attorney—is found brutally raped and murdered. The main clues at the murder scene are a glass with two fingerprints, a sample of semen mixed with spermicidal jelly from a missing diaphragm, and some carpet and hair fibers.

**Conflict and complications:** The story is played out against a background of political intrigue woven into upcoming elections in which two powerful men vie for the top spot of Prosecuting Attorney of the county. Once the murder details have been confirmed, Rusty is assigned by his boss, Raymond Horgan, to oversee the search for Carolyn's killer. The problem is that a few months earlier, Rusty had an affair with Carolyn ... an affair that his wife had found out about. It's not that Sabich didn't love Barbara. It's just that he was (oh so willingly) lured into a liaison that was tempestuous, sexy, and compelling. Sabich knew better, of course. But he was hoisted by the Robin Williams petard that states: "God gave man a brain and a penis, but only enough blood to run one at a time."

At Carolyn's bidding, the affair had ended abruptly, devastating Rusty and leaving him in a state of perpetual turmoil and longing. As the murder investigation proceeds, Rusty is hoping that this affair will remain a secret—a hope that is eventually spoiled ... sorta.

Even though the story is jam-packed with details of political shenanigans, hidden files, found and lost evidence, legal minutiae, political and sexual rivalries, briberies, betrayals, and a foundering marriage, it moves at a lickety-split pace. Throughout this story of layered characters and hidden meanings, Turow teases the reader with hints of fireworks to come. And he never lets us down.

**Climax:** Try as they might, Rusty and several detectives cannot find any solid leads to the killer. Then, in a stunning storm of betrayals, Rusty is accused of the murder. He's shocked to learn that his blood type matches the clues at the crime scene, and the carpet fibers match a carpet like the one in his own home.

**Reversal:** Until this point, Rusty has had the full support of his boss and mentor, Raymond Horgan—especially since another one of the deputy prosecutors named Tom Molto had moved into the political camp of Nico Della Guardia, Horgan's rival for county P.A.

But when Della Guardia wins the election, Horgan goes over to the dark side and he, too, works to convict Sabich of premeditated murder. Desperate to acquit himself, Sabich hires Sandy Stern—a brilliant lawyer and the best attorney he has ever opposed in court.

**Resolution:** The last half of the book involves a trial that's chockablock with insider details, revelations, and insights into the minds of both prosecutors and defense attorneys. Seemingly insignificant crumbs of clues are dropped alongside details of bribery, fingerprint science, the validity of evidence, and what goes on in the judge's chamber and bedroom. And at last, after public and private drama involving shocking examples of pros-ecutorial incompetence (e.g. the glass with the fingerprints is lost and can't be found), Sabich is acquitted of all charges.

**Last moment of suspense:** But wait! There's more! If Rusty Sabich didn't rape and murder Carolyn Polhemus, who did? The answer isn't so clear after Sabich confesses to the reader that the sperm found in the victim's body really was his sperm.

Maybe Sabich is guilty after all. Turow clearly believes that, like life, nothing ever gets tied up with a neat ribbon. But he does offer an explanation to the reader that is both philosophical and factual—one fraught with ambiguity and rationalization that recalls the story of how Icarus longed to fly; but in his need to soar, he moved too close to the sun.

## Back to Basics

Finally, an easy way to lock this fundamental story structure into your imagination is to look at a time-tested children's book. So, to balance all the violence, I'll toss in *Where the Wild Things Are* by Maurice Sendak. This simple story illustrates all the touchstones of classical drama with succinct clarity.

**Inciting incident:** The night Max wears his wolf suit, he makes mischief of one kind or another.

**Conflict and complications:** His mother calls him "Wild Thing!" and Max says, "I'll eat you up." So he's sent to bed without his supper. A forest grows in Max's room and he climbs into a boat and sails to where the Wild Things are.

**Climax:** When the Wild Things gnash their teeth, roll their eyes, and show their terrible claws, Max tames them and proclaims that the wild rumpus should begin.

**Reversal:** When the rumpus stops, Max sends the Wild Things to bed without their supper. He then grows lonely and wants to go home.

**Resolution:** Although the Wild Things beg him to stay, Max sets sail for home.

**Last moment of suspense:** Max returns to the comfort of his room but is scared that his mom is still angry. Then he sees that she's left him his supper and it's still hot, and he knows everything will be all right.

For the cynics among you who mutter, "Yeah, but that's just a kids' book," allow me to remind you that this mere kids' book has been in print for forty-five years, sold more than nineteen million copies, and was the basis of an opera, a major museum exhibition, a ballet, and a feature film. This, by anyone's measure, spells success—a literary and commercial success based on classical storytelling verities.

## THE PAGE-TURNER VS. THE HO-HUM READ

After I began writing my first novel, I took it upon myself to figure out what it was that made me want to keep on reading—what qualities created a page-turner and what techniques contributed to a riveting read.

Since I didn't know diddly-squat about the technical aspects of constructing a novel, I decided to dissect a book that didn't let me put it down. A big-time, gotta-read-it, 3 A.M., can't-close-the-covers page-turner. In this case, I chose Mario Puzo's *The Godfather*, a book I'd read and thoroughly enjoyed but had never analyzed.

For the first time in my writing life, I read a book for strictly technical reasons. I was amazed at what I learned when I brought a consciousness of the author's technique to my reading experience. Little tricks that never occurred to me suddenly popped off the page.

In film, a musical theme or song for the next scene often starts playing before the previous scene ends. A technique first used in a movie called *The Graduate*, the song pulls the viewer forward into the story, connecting one scene to the next with a melodic thread that creates a musical momentum all its own. Puzo does something similar in *The Godfather*.

He structures his story so that he wraps up one storyline in the middle of one chapter and begins another that doesn't end until the middle of a future chapter, 50 or 250 pages down the line.

Obviously, Puzo didn't invent this trick. When Charles Dickens wrote *The Old Curiosity Shop*, it was serialized in a weekly magazine. Each installment was a short, self-contained unit. Yet it also left readers eager to know what would happen next to Little Nell or her friend Kit. One cliffhanger was so exciting that a mob of readers stormed the piers when the next installment of the magazine arrived by ship.

In Puzo's cliffhanger approach, the author never ends a "story" at the end of a chapter. Instead, he leaves a major plot line dangling. The reader can't put the book down at the end of the chapter because there is always some urgent need to find out what's going to happen to Fredo or Sonny or Connie—or even to the Godfather himself. Someone in the Corleone family is always in jeopardy. Or someone who is trying to kill someone who betrayed someone in the Corleone family is in jeopardy.

The bottom line is that there is never a moment in that book when you don't want to know what's going to happen next—or who's the next person to swim with the fishes.

The story lesson from *The Godfather* can be directly applied to your novel, screenplay, or memoir. You can, however, skip the concrete shoes.

## Seven Ways to Make Your Story a Page-Turner

Here are a few tried-and-true ways to keep your story moving and your reader turning pages.

1. **Evoke curiosity.** Provoke the reader's interest. Reveal a secret, generate a plot line, or create a mystery—making sure these elements have consequences further into the story.

2. **Never end at endings.** Avoid ending a plot line at the end of a chapter. That makes it too easy for the reader to put the book down.

3. **Think middle to middle.** Whether you have a short subplot line or an extended one, begin the story in the middle of one chapter and end it in the middle of another.

4. **Pose questions.** Construct your chapter endings so you ask a question instead of answer it.

5. **Remember to remind.** Keep reminding your reader about the problem your character has, the trouble he's in, or the goal he's striving toward that's just out of reach.

6. **Don't forget the villain.** If you've got a villain, use him. Weave him into the story by reminding the reader of the villain's intentions or the hero's fears.

7. **Honor the inevitable.** Remember that what happens next should be inevitable—but not predictable. I'll cover this subject in greater detail in the next chapter.

## 10

# THE END

## ... Or the End of the Beginning?

---

*Begin at the beginning ... and go on till you
come to the end: then stop.*

—Lewis Carroll

Just as it's easier to work a maze backwards, it also helps to know
what and where your ending is when you begin your book.

From the moment you conceive your opening sentence, you
will write with more confidence and move forward with a stronger sense of purpose and a steadier momentum if you have a
general idea of how your story will end. You don't need to know
all the details of the ending. Nor is it necessary to focus on the
fictional destination with every word you write. It's a matter of
maintaining an awareness of your ultimate goal.

When art students learn to draw, they are taught perspective.
In order to indicate perspective, a road made up of two ostensibly
parallel lines grows narrower as it moves toward the horizon
line. Think of your story as that road. And think of your ending

as the precise point at which the two "parallel" lines meet. In order to convey the full depth and distance of your picture, the convergence of the lines brings the story together at one final, inevitable point.

## THE FUNDAMENTALS OF ENDINGS

There are lots of ways to end a book—happy or sad, mysterious or ambivalent, comic or tragic. The first thing to keep in mind about your ending is that it must honor the contract you made with the reader in the opening paragraphs. This doesn't mean the ending must be happy or predictable. But it does mean that the ending must be inevitable.

Whatever ending you choose, you must lead up to it in an honest way. Like Hansel and Gretel, even in the simplest story you must drop enough crumbs for the reader to follow so the ending is a logical outgrowth of the path you have traveled through the book. In other words, you can't spring a surprise on the reader at the last minute that you haven't laid the groundwork for in advance. Whether you're writing a drama, a romance, a thriller, or a mystery, you must lead the reader in an honest way to an inevitable ending. The groundwork might be obscured and the hint might be subtle, but the clues must be there in order to justify the surprise you create.

### Keeping Your Promise

When you make a promise to the reader, it's your obligation to deliver on it in the ending. Anything less than a full payoff is a violation of the author–reader contract.

- If you promise a mystery, end with the solution.

- If you promise action, end with resolution.

- If you promise sin, offer redemption.

- If you promise confusion, end with understanding.

- If you promise anguish, end with relief.

- If you promise humor, end with a punch line.

- If you promise a coming-of-age story, end with insight and growth.

- If you promise a love story, end with a resolved relationship.

The ending of your story doesn't have to be happy or predictable. Nor does it need to be tied up in pretty little bows with everybody smiling and waving goodbye. But it does need to be the inescapable outcome of plot lines and promises you have set up throughout the book. Furthermore, the ending must be played out onstage in full dramatic regalia.

## The Ending as Beginning: Invitation to a Sequel

As certain and inevitable as the ending of a book should be, this does not mean the story stops at this point. In fact, you should do everything you can to convey a sense that the story continues after the reader closes the book—especially if you want to write a series based on the same character. A belief in the future of the characters is one of the primary elements that makes a book memorable.

Presumably, you have created characters who live and breathe, love and hate, rage and submit, desire and avoid, embrace and deny, coax and bluster ... characters whose lives are lived out in all their multiple manifestations and contradictions between the pages of a book. What they were doing before the story began will continue after the story ends. The circumstances of their lives may have changed. The course of their lives might have shifted direction. They might have grown in understanding and depth and character. But they will continue to live their lives in a way that the reader is invited to imagine.

If you structure your endings skillfully, these questions about protagonist and antagonist remain in the reader's mind long after the door is closed on your story.

Readers will embrace your book and look forward to the sequel if you give them the impression that the story doesn't end when it ends. Characters continue to grow and lives continue to evolve. This sense of future possibility creates the longing to know more—the sense of hope that extends beyond the last page of your book.

There should be no question that your story is going to move forward. No question the hero will do her best to live life in the new direction that was set during the course of the story.

That is what makes the ending satisfying and the book worthwhile. And what makes readers come back for more.

Not everyone can write books with an ending that is, in fact, a beginning. It requires writing with enough clarity and confidence to herald the coming of the next book. J.K. Rowling mastered this technique in her Harry Potter series, demonstrated by the fact that the books are some of the best sellers of all time. She created enduring characters and an engaging story that has captivated readers enough to keep coming back. The astonishing success of the series is confirmation of the fact that readers are willing to follow a character through the next book if the previous book leads them to it with skill and intrigue.

In *Harry Potter and the Sorcerer's Stone*, Rowling ends her story in this way:

> "Hope you have—er—a good holiday," said Hermione, looking uncertainly after Uncle Vernon, shocked that anyone could be so unpleasant.
>
> "Oh, I will," said Harry, and they were surprised at the grin that was spreading over his face. "They don't know we're not allowed to use magic at home. I'm going to have a lot of fun with Dudley this summer ...."

There's a distinct sense that some naughty fun awaits the hero. Even if he's not allowed to use his new magical power, Harry is confident he knows how to avoid being a victim at the hands of the wretched Dudley. Needless to say, readers want to share this experience with their hero ... and to learn how Harry's next year at wizard school will play out.

## Life Beyond the Cover of the Book

Even if you're not writing a series, you can increase the chances your reader will remember your character long after the final page by creating an ending that implies the life of the character continues after the reader closes the covers of the book. For instance, Pat Conroy ends *The Prince of Tides* with a sense of loss and longing:

> But it is the secret life that sustains me now, and as I reach the top of that bridge I say it in a whisper, I say it as a prayer, as regret, as praise. I can't tell you why I do it or what it means, but each night when I drive toward my southern home and my southern life, I whisper these words: "Lowenstein, Lowenstein."

And the ending of *Catch-22*, Joseph Heller's mad World War II masterpiece, is steeped in a wild kind of hope.

> "Goodbye, Yossarian," the chaplain called. "And good luck. I'll stay here and persevere, and we'll meet again when the fighting stops."
>
> "So long, Chaplain. Thanks, Danby."
>
> "How do you feel, Yossarian?"
>
> "Fine. No, I'm very frightened."
>
> "That's good," said Major Danby. "It proves you're still alive. It won't be fun."
>
> Yossarian started out. "Yes it will."
>
> "I mean it, Yossarian. You'll have to keep on your toes every minute of every day. They'll bend heaven and earth to catch you."
>
> "I'll keep on my toes every minute."
>
> "You'll have to jump."
>
> "I'll jump."
>
> "Jump!" Major Danby cried.
>
> Yossarian jumped. Nately's whore was hiding just outside the door. The knife came down, missing him by inches, and he took off.

It's worth noting that both of these endings played out with a compelling sense of drama when they were adapted for the screen.

# PITFALLS AND POTHOLES AT THE END OF THE ROAD

Sometimes a writer commits himself to an ending that doesn't work. He has constructed a story that has one inevitable conclusion, but by the time he's written that story, it becomes apparent that the previously planned outcome is a mistake.

As much as I talk about the necessity of the inevitable ending, be prepared to change it if your story leads you in a new direction. Sometimes characters and circumstances lure you onto a different path—one you hadn't planned, but that is ultimately more intriguing and more appropriate. When detours happen, the most important thing to remember is not to shy away from rethinking and rewriting your story to accommodate the new ending. Surprise can be gratifying to both author and reader.

## U-Turns and Detours: A Personal Aside

Every time I make a major revision, I remember the six full drafts of my first novel I typed out on my trusty Smith Corona portable typewriter. Each draft represented at least three or four weeks of rewriting and typing. That doesn't include all the literal cutting and pasting and constructing of new pages with tape and a copy machine.

Compared to the old method, computers make revisions a snap. Cut, paste, insert, rewrite ... no scissors or tape required.

Not long ago I was ghostwriting a book, and in the final, down-to-the-wire edit I realized the outline I had followed so carefully no longer made the sense it did when I set out on the project. The person for whom I wrote the book kept giving me new material that hadn't been factored into the initial concept. These contributions changed the approach I had originally conceived. The deadline was three days away and the manuscript felt overly complicated and confusing.

Instead of crawling under my blankie and hiding (which I was sorely tempted to do), I sat down at my computer and spent three intense days reconfiguring the entire book. I constructed a new framework, eliminated old chapters and sections, and created new ones. I cut and I pasted, then I rewrote old text and tied it all together with new text to bridge the gaps I had created.

I could not have done this on a typewriter. It wouldn't have happened. I would have bowed my head and resigned myself to handing in a book that lacked the clarity it deserved.

With the help of a computer, serious, sweeping revisions are always possible. You should never shy away from them. Nor should you think they are not worth the effort.

No matter how hard or painful the work might be, improving your manuscript is always worth the effort. That said, however, I would emphasize there's a good chance you can spare yourself this massive rewrite trauma if you acquaint yourself in advance with the pitfalls you can encounter at the end of your book. If you put in the effort now, you'll save a lot of time in rethinking, replotting, and rewriting later on.

## FOUR HAZARDS AT THE END OF THE ROAD

As you come to the end of your narrative journey, there are several road hazards to look out for. Considering these issues in advance can save you a lot of time, anguish, and trouble as you wrap up your story.

### I. Dead Ends

Five years ago I edited a novel that a publisher had commissioned. As I read the story, I edited the prose for precision and clarity; tracked the plot and the subplot; made notes in the margins, notes for a critique, and notes in my head. I also followed the progress of the hero who was on an alleged journey toward personal authenticity. By the time I reached the end of the story, I didn't care whether the hero succeeded or failed. I felt as if the publisher and I had wasted a lot of time on a story that didn't work on any level.

Some background—with circumstances disguised, of course: At the beginning of the story, the hero wants to go to a special ski resort where his mother and father don't want him to go. So the young man lies to his parents in order to get there. Without a trace of guilt, the hero travels to the resort, sees his friends, has some adventures, gets into trouble, has his driving emotional problem solved for him by someone else, and returns home. At the end of the book—since his lie goes undetected—the hero tells another lie to his parents in order to travel somewhere else he's not supposed to go.

The hero has learned nothing. He hasn't grown. He hasn't changed. He lacks essential integrity. He'll do anything to get what he wants. He's still a shameless deceiver. So at the end of this novel, why in the world would any reader care about him? And why in the world would someone choose to read another book by this author?

The answer is, they wouldn't.

It probably comes as no surprise that, ultimately, the decision was made not to publish the book.

I offer this editing saga as an example of just about everything you can do wrong in a story. The hero is dishonest; it's hard to cheer for the success of a liar unless he has some serious redeeming features. The hero gets into trouble and someone else gets him out of it, which is not only cheating on the part of the writer, it's disappointing for the reader. Furthermore, the hero doesn't have enough conscience or insight to understand he has done anything wrong.

Beyond those obvious failings, the author constructs a totally unsatisfying ending. If the hero hasn't grown or changed or learned anything, there's not an ending in all of literature that could convince me this novel is worth reading.

At the beginning of this book, once the hero lies to his parents, the implicit contract with the reader states that he will learn something from his mistake. He will grow. He will change. The hero will learn that deceit has its price. Everything points toward that ending. But the author ignores the signs. This leaves the reader feeling angry and dissatisfied and determined never to read another book by this writer.

**Ending Rule #1**: If the hero doesn't change or grow or learn something important, create a new ending or write a new story.

## 2. Speed Demon

You've made your way through a wonderfully constructed, artfully paced novel, only to discover the author has tied up the ending in two pages. You're now left with a sense of *Huh? What happened to the ending? Where'd it go?*

Now you see it, now you don't.

This fictional sin isn't that uncommon. I've seen it time and again. I've done it, too. I suspect the reason this happens is that the author simply grows tired of writing the book. He's busted his literary rear for a solid year or two and he's understandably weary.

I recently critiqued an intriguing and memorable novel with an abrupt and unsatisfying ending. When the author reached the end of the story, he tied up all the loose ends in a flash. Even though the hero was forced to overcome one dreadful thing after another that had been perpetrated by the villain of the story, he never confronted the villain in a final, decisive scene. What confrontation did happen was played out offstage—and the reader was deprived of the satisfaction of watching the hero stand up to his nemesis. It was as if the author couldn't write one more scene with this character. So he tossed the balls in the air and caught them all at once—wrapping up the story in one page.

Resolving the story in an abbreviated flashback or exposing the action of the final scene through one character's dialogue summing up what happened shortchanges the reader. Even the most brilliantly conceived ending played offstage is no substitute for the full dramatization of your big showdown.

**Ending Rule #2:** Always play out your ending on stage.

## 3. Surprise Intersection

Have you ever driven down a road and suddenly come upon an intersection you didn't know was there? Without warning, the side road appears out of nowhere and its presence makes no sense.

The same can be said of amazing coincidence that pops up in a story. Granted, life is full of coincidence. But fiction isn't.

Furthermore, you can't introduce a solution to a problem from out of left field.

Let's say you're writing a mystery that involves a solution the hero can't solve because he doesn't know how to lift fingerprints off a windowsill. So three-quarters of the way through your book when the villain is about to get away with his dastardly deed, your hero runs into a long-lost friend who just happens to know all about fingerprints. By using this coincidence instead of having the hero himself learn about fingerprints, you've just blown the story into disjointed little bits. Again, Charles Dickens might be able to get away with this, but we ordinary mortals cannot.

**Ending Rule #3:** If you haven't prepared the reader in advance for the amazing coincidence, you're not allowed to include it in the story.

## 4. Secret Exit Ramp

In classical Greek drama, when one of the gods was in a major pickle, sometimes Zeus would sweep down on the stage from the wings, pluck the hero out of harm's way, and carry him off to live happily ever after as he cavorts with nubile goddesses in the peaks and meadows of Mount Olympus. This theatrical technique is known as *deus ex machina*—literally, "god from the machine." Consider it the literary equivalent of being saved by the bell.

Children have used *deus ex machina* for ages. Every time they end a story with, "And then Tammy woke up and realized everything was just a dream," they're introducing a contrived, last-minute reprieve into the tale.

Another rabbit-out-of-the-hat situation might be when the villain confronts the hero. Just when things get dicey and the hero is about to be defeated, he reaches into the desk drawer and pulls out a gun. But if the reader doesn't know in advance there's a pistol in the drawer, you can't allow the hero to use it.

The lesson here is simple. Never ask the reader to buy an ending that's built around the sudden entry of a savior—whether that savior is a bell, a hero, or a beast. Even if you hide them well, you must sprinkle foreshadowing plot crumbs for the reader to follow. Not only will the reader not buy the last-minute entrance of the savior, he'll resent the savior's intrusion into the story.

**Ending Rule #4:** No *deus ex machina* allowed.

Study these road hazards. Make them an integral part of your consciousness as you plan your narrative. Writing with an awareness of these four rules will allow you to bring your story to an intelligent, inevitable close with minimum plot pain and maximum creative pleasure. And it will make the process of telling your tale a positive experience for you and a rewarding experience for the reader.

## CLOSING LINES

Read the closing lines from the following books. Then ask yourself:

- What makes these endings work?
- Are these endings effective?
- What do you like or not like about them?
- What makes the endings memorable?
- What feeling are you left with?
- Has the author conveyed the possibility of future action?
- How do you think the story will continue?

*The Maltese Falcon* by Dashiell Hammett:

> She said in a small, flat voice: "Iva is here."
> Spade, looking down at his desk, nodded almost imperceptibly. "Yes," he said, and shivered. "Well, send her in."

*The Catcher in the Rye* by J.D. Salinger:

> About all I know is, I sort of miss everybody I told about. Even old Stradlater and Ackley, for instance. I think I even

miss that goddam Maurice. It's funny. Don't ever tell anybody anything. If you do, you start missing everybody.

*Birdy* by William Wharton:

> "And so what happens then?"
>> "Nothing, Al; just the rest of our lives."
>> "Is that all?"
>> "That's all?"
>> "And that's the way it ends?"
>> "Not really, Al. It's never that easy. Nobody gets off
> that way."
>> But it's worth trying.

*The Godfather* by Mario Puzo:

> Then, with a profound and deeply willed desire to be-
> lieve, to be heard, as she had done every day since the
> murder of Carlo Rizzi, she said the necessary prayers
> for the soul of Michael Corleone.

*The Great Gatsby* by F. Scott Fitzgerald:

> So we beat on, boats against the current, borne back
> ceaselessly into the past.

PART III

# STRUCTURAL SUPPORTS

# 11

# SCENES

## How They're Structured and What Makes Them Work

What is the pattern of a scene? Fundamentally,
it is: Statement of goal. Introduction and
development of conflict. Failure of the character
to reach his goal, a tactical disaster.

—Jack M. Bickham

Now that we've covered the overall framework of a story, it's time to consider the material that fits inside that structure, beginning with scenes.

In all stories, the basic purpose of a scene is simple: to use action and character development to move the reader from one plot point to the next. Think of scenes as stepping stones that steer you down the path of your story. Each stone is separate from the other, yet each is critical to reaching the end of the journey. The stones not only form a larger whole, they lead the reader from the beginning, through the middle, and to the end of the fictional journey.

Some writers view this journey as a process of scene and sequel or action and reaction. For example, something happens: A little girl doesn't return home from school when she's expected. The sequel/reaction might initially involve the parents' response to the absence. Then the responses of school personnel, friends, and law enforcement come into play. These characters not only react to the news of the missing child, but to the actions and reactions of others. In this way, each subsequent scene—or sequel—is built upon reactions to what came before.

Reactions to events come in four basic flavors:

- emotion
- thought
- decision
- action

Stories told in the first-person point of view (see chapter fourteen) tend to elicit reactions that evoke more thought and emotion than a juggernaut thriller. They usually involve healthy doses of self-reflection and internal dialogue, as can be seen in books as different as J.D. Salinger's *The Catcher in the Rye* and Walter Mosley's *Devil in a Blue Dress*.

On the other hand, writers such as Raymond Chandler (*The Big Sleep)* and Tom Clancy *(The Hunt for Red October)* create stories that rely far more on decision and action to fuel their hard-charging plots. Here, the characters—cynical and tough—aren't inclined toward inner examination. Action is their thing.

Just as a story has a beginning, middle, and end, so does each scene.

Some people think of scenes as mini short stories. However, there is one important difference between a story and a scene: The short story has a resolution and conclusion, whereas the scene moves the action forward by avoiding these same elements. Instead of resolution, the end of each scene ratchets up the intensity of the story by asking a question or complicating the plot, thus forcing the reader to move to the following scene in order to find out what happens next.

To accomplish this goal, says James N. Frey—author of *How to Write a Damn Good Novel*—the hero should always emerge from the end of the scene in deeper trouble than when he began.

## A SCENIC OVERVIEW

The following are some basic principles of creating scenes:

- The first scene of the book sets the stage for your story by creating an inciting incident. Something happens— something that demands a response.

- To begin a new scene, pick up where you left off in the last scene, shift to a new situation, or move to the subplot.

- In the middle of your scene the conflict should continue to play out or the complication should increase. This escalating action can be presented either in flashback or in chronological order (see chapter six).

- The end of the scene complicates the situation of the hero and points to future action, thus propelling the reader forward into the next scene.

## THE TEN COMMANDMENTS OF SCENE SENSE

Although the possibilities for scene are endless, there are some basic guidelines you can follow to ensure your readers keep turning the pages. Use these ten as a checklist for evaluating your own scenes.

### I. Honor the Law of Cause and Effect

In a movie, when the camera lingers—even fleetingly—on an object, this is a hint to the viewer that something is afoot, that this object is going to play a role in the story. If it turns out that the object *doesn't* play a part, the viewer is left wondering why the director led him or her astray.

The same concept applies to a book. You shouldn't present a situation that drops a hint about a possible future action without following up on it. I hasten to add that you don't need to follow up in the next scene. But sooner or later, if you create a cause, you should have an effect. Think Sir Isaac Newton's Third Law of Motion: For every action there is an equal and opposite reaction.

Readers are astute. They will remember you implied that Andrew has been having an affair or that Damon's father is a detective in the drug division of the LAPD—especially if the main characters are smoking dope. Both of these statements, no matter how casual, demand a follow-up. To ignore them is to break your contract with the reader.

## 2. Create Credible Motivation

Konstantin Stanislavski was the founding father of "The Method," the technique promoted by Lee Strasberg at the Actor's Studio in New York to train actors ranging from Marlon Brando and Montgomery Clift to Meryl Streep and Daniel Day-Lewis. Stanislavski emphasized that actors should discard conventional stage technique and, instead, break down the text of the drama by looking at the character's motivations. The actor could then apply his own personal experience to the role, thus formulating more genuine actions and reactions to the unfolding drama.

The Method—satirized by Dustin Hoffman in *Tootsie*—has caused a lot of people to roll their eyes when an actor asks, "What's my motivation?" They think questions such as this are pretentious or, worse, silly. And yet attention must be paid to this very issue. Strasberg maintained that dynamic acting demands "belief, faith, and imagination." The same could be applied to writing.

In fiction, characters do not function in a vacuum. They don't suddenly do something that hasn't been foreshadowed or for which the reader hasn't been prepared. Linda can't cheat on her driver's test without the author creating motivation for her behavior. Maybe she's dyslexic or couldn't study for the test because she had a fight with her husband. Whatever the reason—or reasons—for her behavior, sooner or later, Linda's motivations for her actions must be justified.

As you write, ask yourself if your character's actions are credible. Given this person's background, personality, and inclinations, is this action or thought or decision believable? If it is not, either remove the action or rewrite previous scenes to set up this scene.

## 3. Avoid Dead Ends

When you write your scene, remember that you must move from point A to point B. You cannot begin at point A and finish in the same place at the end of the scene. If the action hasn't been advanced in some way, the scene doesn't belong in the book.

Besides avoiding resolution, there is one basic way to avoid a dead end: point to future action. If you begin a scene with the hero coming upon a treasure, you don't want to end the scene with him staring at the treasure chest. Some forward action must be implied, otherwise the story remains static. (*Go on, hero. Open it!*)

Once that chest is open, we have a whole world of conflict to choose from: Is the hero going to zip his lips and try to find out who the treasure belongs to? Is he going to keep the treasure a secret so he can share it with his girlfriend? Or is the hero going to call the authorities? There are lots of possibilities—even the hero's confusion about what to do can be one of them. The rule here is, make certain you imply future action before the scene ends.

## 4. Maintain Credibility

One of the great struggles writers face in developing believable stories is creating plots that grow out of a plausible premise and characters that behave in credible ways. When it comes to outstanding storytelling, it's all about what Samuel Taylor Coleridge called "the willing suspension of disbelief."

In a variation on the man with the treasure chest, let's say you're writing a story about a young man from a small town in

Oklahoma who visits his grandparents in New York City. One night he looks out his window and sees two thugs burying a box in the empty lot next door. Even though he was raised on a farm and lives in the Back of Beyond, the onlooker is no dummy. He knows big city street gangs are tough and ruthless. But instead of telling his grandparents or calling the police, the hero decides to take on the two hardened New York street toughs single-handedly. He follows the bad guys and confronts them. When they object to his attention, he beats the daylights out of them.

Gimme a break. Not credible.

You cannot introduce a surprise, last-minute "fix" for your story. You must have a credible reason for the guy to play superhero. You've got to establish the fact that he's spent the last seven years earning his black belt in karate or mastering advanced techniques of Krav Maga—and that he thinks the guys may be burying something that was stolen from his grandmother.

In a nutshell: The action in a scene must be a credible consequence of previous occurrences—not the result of the character doing something no sane person would ever do or of a last-minute fix or add-on to the plot.

## 5. Keep Your Eye on the Goal
Sometimes a scene opens with a dynamite plot point, then gets lost in the narrative woods. Failure to keep action moving forward is one of the fundamental mistakes a writer can make.

As you write, ask yourself if you are moving steadily toward the end of the scene, the end of the chapter, and the end of the story. If your plot or subplot threads move in too many directions, you impede the narrative momentum.

In fact, if a scene meanders aimlessly, the reader will lose patience and lose focus. He might even lose interest in the book altogether. Then he'll donate it to the next sale at the local library instead of keeping it and recommending it to his friends at college, where his professor would hear about it and praise your story on a special Web site for writing students—thus increasing your sales exponentially and catapulting your book onto the best-seller list just below the latest Walter Mosley. This gets the best-seller list just below the latest Walter Mosley. This gets you the most prominent agent in the business who negotiates a deal for the sale of your next book for $500,000. And that book wins the Pulitzer Prize.

That is what I mean by losing sight of your goal.

## 6. Remind the Reader of the Central Conflict

Conflict lives in the heart and soul of a plot. If the reader forgets what is driving the hero, she won't care enough about him to finish the book.

It's not good enough to open your story with your character becoming embroiled in a first-rate, complex, mind-boggling conflict. If you don't remind the reader of this complication at frequent intervals and ratchet up the intensity of those complications in multiple scenes, you will lose the momentum of the story.

Suppose Molly's goal is to get the lead in an off-Broadway play. Her best friend Fiona also wants that role. So the central conflict is that Molly is torn between her personal ambition and her loyalty to her friend. Auditions for the play are three weeks away. In the meantime, Molly and Fiona wait tables in the same restaurant, attend acting classes, and go to the movies together. But never once during these three weeks do they discuss the auditions. Never once is the reader reminded that Molly is torn between loyalty and ambition. At the end, the two women try out for the play and they are both so good they are allowed to play the roles on alternate nights.

Ho-hum. Big yawn.

By avoiding the conflict of interests—rivalry, regret, jealousy, fear, anxiety, confrontation, confusion—we cut out the heart of the story, remove the drama from the relationship between the two women, and blunt the reader's interest.

Instead of playing it safe, consider the storytelling lessons classic comic books offer us. Year in and year out, Lex Luthor lurks in Superman's background and the Joker haunts Batman's psyche. Neither the reader nor the fictional hero is ever allowed to forget that a confrontation with the nemesis is waiting just around the next corner. This critical push–pull relationship between hero and villain is what drives the stories and maintains the reader's interest.

## 7. Conjure Up Interesting Obstacles

If conflict is the engine that drives the plot, obstacles are the fuel that propels the conflict. The hero's struggle to overcome the obstacles you set before him invites the emotional investment of the reader. Without the reader cheering for the success of the hero, the story falls flat and becomes a bland reading experience.

Going back to Molly in the play: Instead of competing for the starring role with her friend, suppose Molly has a speech impediment. She has been working with a speech teacher and wants to prove to her friends and her family that she can stand up on stage and speak at least one line without stuttering.

When Molly's brother hears she's going to audition for the play, he teases her by wishing her "gggg-ood l-lllluck." When her parents hear what she's about to do, they gently suggest she try secretarial school instead. And when her best friend hears about the audition plans, she tries to save Molly from embarrassment. But in spite of all the roadblocks, Molly perseveres. She overcomes one obstacle after another, and in the end, she prevails. At the audition, she recites her lines perfectly without a hesitation or a stutter.

On the other hand, today—with the advent of more realistic and nuanced endings—the story might even conclude with Molly repeating her lines with a stutter. Here, the triumph lies in the hero finding the courage to stand up and speak before an audience.

Molly confronting and overcoming obstacles—not her desire to act in the play or her triumph on opening night—is the action that fuels the story.

With this in mind, set up your scenes so that obstacles are presented in one scene but not resolved until future scenes. This kind of literary steeplechase—jumping over a puddle here and a hurdle there—is what keeps the plot moving forward and keeps the reader's interest from flagging.

## 8. Take Two Steps Forward, One Step Backward

Just because the hero makes discernible progress toward his goal in one scene, do not allow him to move forward unimpeded in the following scenes. Overcoming one obstacle after another without a setback makes for dull reading.

Think *Rocky*, the story of a two-bit boxer who, by dint of his name alone, ends up in a match against heavyweight champion Apollo Creed. For Rocky—who makes up in grit what he lacks in confidence—the road to the title fight is filled with challenges. He's underweight and underprepared. But he's determined to go the distance with Creed—i.e., last fifteen rounds in the ring without collapsing. Nobody takes Rocky seriously. Not even Rocky.

At the beginning of the fight, Rocky knocks Creed down. And then, of course, Creed knocks Rocky down. That's when the bout gets serious and the hero gets battered. His eye is cut and it swells shut. But Rocky continues to stagger and fight. Two steps forward, one step back. All the way through the climax of the movie, the hero struggles to overcome obstacles in order to achieve his goal. Rocky's response to these events—his setbacks and his determination to prove he's just not another bum—is what makes conflict interesting and the story worth reading.

## 9. Increase the Tension by Raising the Stakes

A playwright ratchets up the tension in a scene when he has two actors confront each other. At first, Rick wants to read the letter Maida is holding because he's curious about who wrote it. Then his motivation to get the letter intensifies when he realizes the letter Maida holds contains unkind remarks he wrote about her.

You can approach this scene in a different way if you shift the point of view. At first Maida is merely annoyed with Rick because she's heard he said something untrue about her. When she actually reads the letter, she shifts into what my mother used to call a double-dyed duck fit. In both situations, the goal is the same: to intensify the experience by upping the ante and revealing information one piece at a time.

If your character is moving toward a goal and every obstacle he overcomes constitutes the same level of difficulty, the story becomes less and less interesting.

Think of your obstacles as Olympic events. The first obstacle the hero confronts may only rate a "three" on the predetermined level of difficulty. But by the end of the climax, the hero should have vaulted over an obstacle that's a solid and impressive "ten."

## 10. Simplify Your Scene's Players

Do not use one more person in your scene than absolutely necessary. Consider this: In the opening scene of a book, two young men are hanging out on the corner. Pierre says something. George responds. They go at it. Instead of staying focused on the two combatants, the focus shifts to the reactions of bystanders. As the fight escalates, Sam says something, then Charles adds his two cents worth. Abby backs off and starts to run. And when Brad hears a siren, he jumps over a fence and disappears.

This is not the stuff of good fiction. Who's the protagonist here? Where should the reader's attention be focused? Are all these people necessary to the story? Much better to have the guys isolated in the corner of the basketball court and tell the story of the conflict from one point of view. Whether that point of view is from one of the fighters or from an onlooker is up to you.

When you overcomplicate a scene, the reader is forced to spend unnecessary effort trying to figure out what's happening and why, which character is which, who's doing what to whom, what the purpose of the scene is, and how the story is unfolding. Tracking extraneous complications is not only annoying, it creates an intrusion in the narrative, which breaks the narrative spell you've worked so hard to cast. The rule here is: simplify.

## TRICKS OF THE TRADE
### Pacing Your Stakes

As you construct your plot points, take care not to raise the stakes too high too soon. If you do this, you can't escalate the action to a plausible height when you reach the climax of the story. I once heard a (probably apocryphal but nevertheless relevant) story about a mystery writer who killed off so many people in so many horrific ways by page 50, he reached the point where there was no kind of credible mayhem he could create—short of dropping a bomb—to top his previous murders. There was no more story to tell. The only thing the author could do was return to Go and start over again—this time with only two victims biting the dust in the same number of pages.

So the lesson here is: Save your finale for the finale.

## CONSTRUCTING AND CONNECTING SCENES

You'll do yourself a big favor if you begin your book with an opening scene that foreshadows future action. Not only does it hook the reader by promising imminent conflict, it makes the writer's job so much easier when it comes to connecting to the next scene and the next.

Consider the opening sentence of Mario Puzo's novel *The Godfather*:

> Amerigo Bonasera sat in New York Criminal Court Number 3 and waited for justice: vengeance on the men who had so cruelly hurt his daughter, who had tried to dishonor her.

This scene goes on for a page and a half, showing how the judge gives the men who harmed the young woman a suspended sentence. And the scene ends with an outraged and hate-filled Bonasera turning to his wife and saying, "They have made fools of us ... For justice we must go on our knees to Don Corleone."

There's nothing too flashy here. A man seeks justice under the law, and when he doesn't get it, he determines how he will get it in spite of the law. Begging is inevitable. Violence is implied. And readers are hooked.

The next scene shifts to a drunken, has-been singer named Johnny Fontane confronting his trampy wife. She taunts him, then leaves him sprawled on the floor as she disappears into the bedroom. The scene ends with a desperate Fontane deciding to return to New York.

> He would go back to the one man with the power, the wisdom, he needed and a love he still trusted. His Godfather Corleone.

And in the third scene of chapter one, a baker named Nazorine confronts a young Italian POW named Enzo who is smitten with the baker's daughter. The only solution to saving his daughter's honor before she gets knocked up is to secure American citizenship for Enzo. And, picking up the recurring theme, the scene ends with these lines:

> And there was only one man who could arrange such an affair. The Godfather. Don Corleone.

In three brief scenes, Puzo establishes that the Godfather has power—both brute and political—and that he also has compassion. The author also points to future action (the results of these three men's petitions to the Godfather), which is a critical way to open your book.

The lengthy first chapter moves on to a long scene at the wedding of Don Corleone's daughter at which the Godfather's power is firmly established in the mind of the reader. And then, in the last scene of the chapter, we are brought full circle. The two young men who dishonored Amerigo Bonasera's daughter are worked over by three of the Godfather's emissaries armed with spiked brass knuckles and spine-cracking kicks.

Scene by scene, all the intrigues and actions of the plot come together as the Godfather's preeminent power is established. The individual scenes of the first chapter—stepping stones on the long path leading inevitably toward the end of the story—have been joined in a greater and more satisfying whole, each piece of the puzzle evoking new curiosity and implying future action as it is established in the reader's mind.

This, then, is how scenes are strung together. Once you understand the big picture, the challenge becomes how to write each individual scene.

## Entering the Scene Mid-Party

Sometimes constructing a scene presents a special problem. Beginners, especially, find it difficult to move into the action.

When I was writing my first novel, I spent an entire day stewing over an important scene that was going to take place at a party.

I tried opening with the arrival of the first guest. I tried opening with the doorbell ringing. Then I tried opening with people emerging from a taxi in front of the apartment building. I wrote the scene every way I could think of in order to move my main character into that party.

Around tea time—screaming with frustration—I stood up from the desk, stomped out the door, and hightailed it down the street to my friend Terry Baker's house. After explaining the dilemma to Terry and telling her that every party opener I'd tried turned into a colossal bore within two paragraphs, Terry looked at me and said, "But Nancy, you don't have to begin at the beginning."

Pause.

"Huh?"

*"You don't have to begin at the beginning."*

"What do you mean?"

"It's called *in medias res*. Latin for 'into the midst of things.' Instead of beginning at the beginning, you start in the middle of the scene ... in the middle of the party."

Brain kicks into gear.

Light goes on.

"So *that's* how it's done," I say.

There you have it. Major *aha!* moment for me. Everything I needed to know about a scene but didn't have the sense to ask. After falling to my knees in gratitude, I hustled home, sat down at the typewriter, and opened my scene with the character planted in the middle of the action in the middle of the party.

This common-sense approach may seem obvious to some writers. But I'd never taken a writing class. And I'd never read a book on writing. I was an untutored novice, and this *in medias res* thing was certainly not obvious to me. Once I got a handle on this simple concept, however, my novel moved forward at a much more satisfying pace.

## Two points about the mid-party technique

**1. You must play catch-up.** It may not be immediately apparent, but if you begin the scene in the middle of the action, you're going to have to play a little catch-up with the reader.

For instance, I open a scene with Mary at a yoga retreat as she meditates for the first time. This occurs after Mary has told her husband in the previous scene that even though she's a wreck, she absolutely refuses to go to Camp Tranquility. Instead of chanting "ohmms" around the campfire, Mary wants to stay home and work toward a delusional goal she's set for herself: i.e., once she loses fifteen pounds, everything will be hunky dory.

After plopping Mary down in the middle of the retreat, sooner or later, I have to double back and explain to the reader what happened to make Mary change her mind about going to the retreat. Did she learn that her blood pressure was dangerously high? Did she decide that learning how to calm her mind was worth deferring her goal? Or did her husband, exhausted from living with her anxiety and distress, bribe her with a promise of a trip to the Bahamas?

**2. You can delay but not deny an explanation.** While you owe your reader an explanation of the hero's motivations, the reader is kept in suspense until you give that explanation—a distinct advantage of the *in medias res* technique.

In other words, you don't have to explain immediately why Mary changed her mind about not going to camp. Delaying the explanation is a legitimate way to pique curiosity, increase tension, and intensify reader involvement. But you do have to explain eventually, or the arc of the story and the motivation of the hero become obscured.

Although this technique is a terrific way to create additional suspense, it can grow tiresome if it's overused. Too many mid-scene entrances followed by too many delayed plot explanations can tick off a reader. A reader can only wonder about what happened to Mary for so long without losing patience. Consequently, don't depend on this ploy for every other scene. Save this technique for your juiciest moments. That way you delay the action and increase the suspense when the reader is most eager to find out what happens next.

Addendum: As with any writing technique, the line between use and over-use is blurry. This is a case, I think, in which you trust your gut. So if knowledge of the reason Mary goes on the retreat is critical to understanding her motivation, then, by all means, answer the question sooner rather than later.

On the other hand, if delaying the answer establishes the story arc and instigates the forward momentum—for instance, if the reason Mary goes to the retreat determines the throughline of the book—then it's legitimate to hold out on the answer until later, even until the end.

So the hard-and-fast rule is that there's no hard-and-fast rule. Use the technique when it enhances the story, piques curiosity, and establishes a story arc. It can be an effective way to add layers to your story.

## Scenus Interruptus

Interrupting the forward action—a kissing cousin to *in medias res*—is a perfect way to ratchet up the suspense in a novel. Let's say you plop Lia right in the middle of the action. She lives in the English countryside with her aged father. He's not only ailing; on his good days, he's a bully and on his bad days, he's a tyrant. When Lia goes to the market one Saturday morning, she meets and falls in love with Devon, the charming lad who lives in the manor house at the top of the hill. After a few months, he invites her to dinner, their first evening alone.

The problem is, Lia's father and Devon's father have a long-standing feud, and there is no way her father will allow her to go. Her father caught her speaking to Devon early on. He told her then that he would rather see her a spinster than have her marry that man. Daddy also warned her that if she tries to see Devon again, he will ship her off to America to live with his sister.

So ... what happens next?

Lia knows if she pulls a Houdini act one more time and gets caught, it's curtains. She'll get shipped off to America and live with her wretched aunt who paints porcelain as a hobby. Could anything be more boring? And really, all she wants to do is meet her soul mate for dinner ... after which they will fall in love and elope to Gretna Green, then move to London—away from her tyrant father—where she and Devon will have three children and live happily ever after.

So Lia decides to sneak out of the house to meet the love of her life. And we open with the young maiden halfway down the ladder. At the bottom, her father waits to whisk her away to her room where he will lock her in until he secures her passage to America.

What's going to happen when our intrepid heroine steps onto the ground and turns around to see Daddy standing there?

You might be eager to find out what happens next, but you'll have to cool your jets. Because we're not going there just yet. We're ending the scene mid–ladder. We're gonna make you sweat while you wait for your story gratification.

We have a couple of options here. We can flash back or we can move to another part of the plot and see what's happening in that neck of the woods.

### The flashback scene
Instead of moving the action forward, midway down the ladder Lia gets scared about what she's doing. That's when we flash back to seven years earlier.

She remembers meeting her aunt at a family reunion when she was just fifteen. Her mother was still alive then. Aunt Glenna Belle meant well, but she was proper and boring and talked way too much. Furthermore, she lived in Texas, a place so alien that the thought of living there made Lia gag.

"Oh God, please spare me a life like that," Lia had told her mother at the time.

And her mother had agreed.

Before the flashback to the wretched family reunion, Lia was about to hop onto the ground at her father's feet, risking exile to the very place, and with the very person, that so horrified her.

The reader is forced to move through the flashback before he can discover what happens next. Only then does Lia turn around and see her father standing there. Until that moment, the reader is kept in suspense.

A reminder: Don't forget to create a solid anchor for the return of the flashback. Readers need clarity about where they've come from in the story and where they are in the action. For instance, you can let the reader know that Daddy's standing at the bottom of the ladder, even though Lia's unaware of his presence. That piece of knowledge makes the scene memorable enough for the reader to want to return to it even though the flashback intervenes.

### The shift to the other side of the plot

We end the scene with Lia climbing down the ladder and her father waiting at the bottom. And instead of shifting into a flashback to her first meeting with her aunt, or carrying the action forward with Lia, we shift to a new point of view and pick up the next scene with Lia's intended, Devon, who awaits her at the end of the lane.

In the meantime, Lia is left clutching the ladder with her father waiting for her.

If Lia doesn't get to the park in time, Devon will leave without her. Then she will miss the opportunity to marry the only man she will ever love.

You get the drift. Double back. Shift focus. Interrupt the main action. By doing so, you increase the suspense and leave the reader with a major question dangling in his head.

## NARRATIVE CONTINUITY

Whatever strategy you use to increase suspense, always remember to maintain the narrative continuity of your story by orienting the reader in time and space. When you reconnect with the main plot, include a prompt about where you are. A simple reminder will do.

Return for one last moment to Lia on the ladder. All you need to do to indicate the return to the present is to create a situation that makes Lia grip the sides of the ladder. This can be accomplished in muted tones. You needn't make a big deal.

> Reliving her visit to Texas—as flat and boring as Aunt Glenna Belle—increased Lia's determination to marry Devon. As soul-numbing as that experience was, living without her love would *definitely* be worse than exile abroad, she thought. The mere idea of her father sending her to America made her grip the sides of the ladder even harder.
>
> One more step and I'm outta here, she thought as she stepped onto the ground ...

There are lots of techniques for story construction, and many more for inventing characters, creating settings, and increasing tension. But it all begins at the beginning with the fundamental building blocks of storytelling and the techniques for mastering the scene.

## SCENE CHECKLIST

Because we've covered so much scenic ground in this chapter, here's a summary that might be helpful. As you write your scenes, keep the following guidelines in mind:

- Point toward future action in the opening scenes.

- Remember that you don't have to begin a scene at the beginning of the action.

- Construct your scenes with action and reaction.

- Create obstacles.

- Avoid dead ends.

- Eliminate gimmicks.

- Raise the stakes.

- Surprise the reader with plausible actions that don't conform to expectations.

# 12

# THE DYNAMIC DUOS
## Story and Quest, Plot and Subplot

---

*A story is a tale with a beginning, a middle, and
an end. It's a quest ... Whether it's returning
to Kansas (Dorothy in* The Wizard of Oz*)
or killing the witch (*Hansel and Gretel*), this
journey is the story, the plot, the means by
which your characters' strengths and weaknesses
are unveiled, his or her lessons learned.*

—Barbara Shapiro

Looking at plot through the lens of classical drama is just one way to envision your story. If the pyramid approach doesn't appeal to you, try dividing your narrative into three separate acts or taking your character on the Hero Quest. All of these time-tested methods are equally effective when it comes to constructing story. Your task is to find the one that works for you.

As you examine each plan, remember that, above all, characters not only define the heart of story, they also make that story memorable.

## THE TRUTH IN STORY

In the purest sense, character *is* story.

What happens to characters—how they suffer and celebrate, how they meet challenges, overcome obstacles, and find redemption—constitutes the heart and soul of story.

All powerful stories contain an essential core of personal truth—some essence drawn from real life that connects fictional awareness with a writer's direct or secondhand experience. This truth needn't mirror the concrete world. Perhaps it's an emotional truth, a spiritual one, that resonates with the writer and forms the core of a story. Or perhaps this truth is an unconscious one, an association and motivation not fully understood at the beginning.

I belong to the school that believes novels like Joseph Heller's *Catch-22*, Tim O'Brien's *Going After Cacciato*, and James Jones's *The Thin Red Line* tell a deeper truth about war than nonfiction books like Cornelius Ryan's *The Longest Day* or even William Manchester's *Goodbye, Darkness*. Both nonfiction accounts are brilliant; they convey the historical sweep and drama of major events in World War II. Nevertheless, it is fiction that has the capacity to illuminate, to touch a reader on not only an intellectual level but a visceral one. It is that truth—deep and layered and passionate—that great storytellers express.

And it is the uncovering of this truth—the search, the investigation, the examination—that makes a story compelling.

### Fiction vs. Fact

Sometimes knowledge of real life is enlightening. Other times it's inhibiting.

Several years ago when I taught at the Big Sur Writing Workshop, a woman read the manuscript of her book about a young man's experience in his first year of medical school—a story based on real life. The characters were interesting, but the story was flat.

Five different writers sitting around the table suggested ways to beef up the story, to inject some life into its essentially dull plot. The problem was, for every suggestion offered, the author countered with, "But that's not the way it happened."

Which brings me to one of the most fundamental issues of writing fiction: *You are creating a story, not recording history.* If you are to fashion an effective plot, you must discard the facts as you know them in the service of a larger truth. Taking this risk is the only way to make the leap into a story that reflects the reality you know, as well as the world you imagine.

## FOUR BASIC CONFLICTS

In fiction, as in life, there are four basic kinds of conflict a character can confront. Although there can be two or three kinds of conflict in the same story, one usually dominates the plot.

### 1. Man Against Man

This conflict covers a lot of stories, from Western gunfights to romances to war stories. It may be the most obvious of conflicts, but the near endless variation of the story—along with the near endless variation of conflicts man has with man—still make for compelling stories.

A classic example is the epic novel *Les Misérables* by Victor Hugo. It tells the story of Jean Valjean, who is convicted of stealing a loaf of bread to feed his starving sister and her children. After nineteen years in prison, Valjean is released, only to find that his past continues to haunt him. Desperate to escape the chains of his former life, he assumes a new identity and, with it, starts a new life as an upstanding citizen.

But the disappearance does not stop the obsessive Inspector Javert from stalking Valjean, mercilessly dogging the man's steps over a period of more than fifteen years. After several twists of fate, Javert confronts the hero for the last time. He is then faced with the terrible choice of upholding the law or upholding the law of morality. Unable to cope in a world not painted in black and white, Javert drowns himself in the Seine.

## 2. Man Against Nature

Since the dawn of time, man has been struggling against nature. It is probably our most primal conflict. This plays out in many ways: man vs. dinosaur in *Jurassic Park*, man vs. shark in *Jaws*, or man vs. the island in *Lord of the Flies*.

*The Perfect Storm* is Sebastian Junger's reconstruction of how the fishing crew of the Andrea Gail battles a massive Atlantic storm in 1991. The six fishermen do not survive. But Junger's re-creation of characters who were on that boat is so compelling that their struggle to battle hundred-foot waves and hurricane-force winds has become a classic of the man against nature genre.

## 3. Man Against Society

Man pitted against society is in every struggle against the government, fight for civil rights, or push for change.

Harper Lee's *To Kill a Mockingbird* is a perfect example of this genre. Set in Alabama during the Great Depression, the book tells the story of a white lawyer named Atticus Finch who is assigned to defend Tom Robinson, a black man accused of raping a white woman. To the horror of the town, Atticus actually defends Tom; he doesn't, in the fine Southern tradition of the time, merely pretend to do so.

Narrated by Finch's six-year-old daughter Scout, the story is a touching and painful exploration of the ramifications and consequences of prejudice in the deep South. And it is also a powerful story of what happens to an honorable man when he is faced with the choice of defending tradition or defending justice.

## 4. Man Against Self

Choice is most painful when there is an equal pull in two directions. And memorable choice is often created out of a war between the heart and head ... or between good and evil.

Like it or not, we all have shadow sides. That dark part of our nature often manifests in moments of stress (see chapter two). Confronting that nature is not only a way to make a character interesting. It is a way to make a character come alive.

The story of self pitted against self is a time-honored literary tradition. In *The Strange Case of Dr. Jekyll and Mr. Hyde*, Robert Louis Stevenson explored the dual nature of man in a story about a doctor tormented by a split personality. Here, the respectable Dr. Jekyll concocts a potion that does not work as anticipated. Instead of evoking the good side of the good doctor, the formula evokes his dark side, an aspect of his personality that becomes increasingly addictive and difficult to reject. Each time Jekyll swallows the potion, he becomes a maniacal killer named Mr. Hyde, a man who thrills to the power of darkness.

Eventually, Hyde no longer returns to his former self. The tormented Jekyll is permanently stuck in the body and mind of a monster. Understanding that he is doomed to live out his life as the personification of evil, he kills himself ... but only after leaving a confession letter behind that explains what has happened to him.

As you examine each conflict scenario to determine which approach creates the greatest benefit for your particular plot requirements, never forget that, above all, "man" is the foundation of each of these stories. In other words, the characters not only define the heart of story, they also make that story memorable.

## STORY IN THREE ACTS

When you create story and characters, your challenge is to find a way for them to inhabit their own unique world while still honoring the verities of storytelling. Plays and movies, novels and narrative nonfiction all feature three basic acts.

The three-act concept is a variation on beginning, middle, and end. Looking at your plot through the lens of three acts is just another way for you to consider the fundamentals of story.

Consider, for instance, *The Graduate,* Mike Nichols's film classic based on a novel by Charles Webb, with the screenplay written by Buck Henry and Calder Willingham. The story epitomizes the agonies of that bewildered rite of passage from extended adolescence to the adult world. Even though the movie is over forty years old, it feels as fresh today as the day it was first released.

## Act I: Problem and Obstacle

In the first act of the movie, Benjamin Braddock (Dustin Hoffman) arrives at the airport, accompanied by the music of Simon and Garfunkel's "The Sounds of Silence" ... "Hello, Darkness my old friend, I've come to talk with you again ..." Since Ben has just graduated from college with high honors and a low sense of direction, this opening scene sets the mood of the movie.

Shortly after his arrival home in Pasadena, his mother and father throw a party for him that he suffers through, doing his best to escape well-meaning parental friends offering career advice for an alienating world epitomized by the iconic "Plastics."

At the end of the party, the wife of his father's law partner, played by Anne Bancroft, asks Benjamin to drive her home. Here, another scene embellished by "The Sounds of Silence" is burned into the imaginations of multiple generations of filmgoers: Mrs. Robinson seducing Ben, shot from the angle beneath her perfectly shaped leg as she removes her stocking.

Ben succumbs to Mrs. Robinson's allure throughout most of the summer. The central problem of the story crops up when Ben meets and falls in love with Mrs. Robinson's daughter Elaine (played by Katherine Ross). This obstacle, of course, constitutes the big *oops* of the story.

Ben wants to date Elaine, which—understandably—pisses off Mrs. Robinson, who threatens to expose his double-dipping ways to her daughter.

## Act II: Conflict or Struggle

In the second act, Benjamin comes face-to-face with the consequences of his actions—creating escalating conflicts in the mother-lover-daughter triangle. Here, the question becomes can Ben achieve his goal despite the formidable obstacles that litter his path: Mrs. Robinson's fury and Elaine's wrath and devastation when she discovers the truth.

In classic second-act style, the plot should have at least three major obstacles or challenges for the hero to overcome, each one more difficult than the one before. *The Graduate* meets the challenge.

- Mrs. Robinson makes Ben promise he won't date Elaine.

- Ben's parents push him to ask the Robinsons' beautiful daughter for a date.

- Ben capitulates and takes Elaine on the date from hell. Afterward, he feels so guilty about his rude attempts to push her away that he apologizes to her, kisses her, and ends up falling in love.

Act II ends with the conflict at its peak: Mrs. Robinson forces Ben to confess to Elaine that he's having an affair with her mother. This devastates Elaine, who then succumbs to her father's will and moves back to Berkeley, where she's in school.

## Act III: Resolution

In the last act, the hero finds a way out of his dilemma and takes the final step toward resolving his problems. The third act opens with Ben following Elaine around the college campus, asking her time and again to marry him. Elaine's father intervenes and she ultimately agrees to marry a dull but acceptable young man named Carl.

Once Ben learns about the impending marriage, he is transformed from his Act I indecisiveness into a daring young man.

In the last scenes of the last act, *The Graduate* presents yet another iconic moment in film history: Fueled by Simon and Garfunkel's "Mrs. Robinson," Benjamin sets out on a desperate drive to Santa Barbara in his red Alfa Romeo in order to stop Elaine from marrying the other man. He runs out of gas, gets lost, and finally makes a mad dash the last few blocks to the church.

And when he arrives, the doors are locked. In a scene forever engraved in movie memory, Ben pounds on the glass of the church window yelling "Elaine! Elaine!" After an excruciating wait, the bride finally turns away from the altar and yells "Ben!"

Chaos erupts, and the stunned groom is left at the altar as Ben and Elaine dash from the church and hop a ride on a bus where they begin their happily confused ever after life together—accompanied by "The Sounds of Silence," bringing the movie full circle with this theme song.

So there you have it: Act I, Problem and Obstacle; Act II, Conflict or Struggle; Act III, Resolution. Whether you're crafting fiction or nonfiction, the fundamentals of these three acts form the basis of story. When it comes to how you present your material, there's lots of wiggle room here. But when it comes to creating the foundation of your story, the three-act convention serves as a rock-solid guide for the challenging fictional journey you're about to undertake.

## THE HERO QUEST

When you consider that character is story, it makes sense that the Hero Quest forms the backbone of plot. This is the universal adventure, the journey—psychological, physical, or emotional—that we take in both literature and life when we set out in search of knowledge and wisdom.

In Greek Myth, Odysseus endures seven years of imprisonment and then overcomes a series of perils—from the threat of the Cyclops to the lure of the Sirens—before he finally returns home to his beloved wife Penelope. In the Old Testament, Jonah is cast into the sea and lives in the belly of the whale for three days before he repents and is vomited out onto dry land.

Just as Orpheus descends into the Underworld to find his beloved Eurydice, the conventions of the Hero Quest demand that the hero descend into darkness before he walks once more in the light.

Just because those stories originated in ancient tales doesn't make their form irrelevant today. Think *Star Wars*, *The Spy Who Came in From the Cold*, *Raiders of the Lost Ark*, and *The Catcher in the Rye*. Also *The Kite Runner*, *To Kill a Mockingbird*, and, of course, *Jane Eyre*. In all of these stories—both simple and complex—the hero travels into the depths in order to find himself. And when he emerges, he is transformed.

In *Hero With a Thousand Faces,* Joseph Campbell says, "Whether the hero be ridiculous or sublime, Greek or barbarian, gentile or Jew, his journey varies little in essential plan. Popular tales represent the heroic action as physical; the high religions show the deed to be moral; nevertheless, there will be found astonishingly little variation in the morphology of the adventure, the character roles involved, the victories gained."

Campbell goes on to say that "if one of the basic elements of the archetypal pattern is omitted from a given fairy tale, legend, ritual, or myth, it is bound to be somehow or other implied." For instance, if the hero doesn't actually go into the underworld as Orpheus does in his search for Eurydice, he has an experience that serves as a stand-in for the underworld—an emotional breakdown, a perilous encounter, or in the words of the mystic, St. John of the Cross, an encounter with "the dark night of the soul." Whether metaphorically or physically, each step of the journey must be played out in the Hero Quest.

## The Six Stages of the Hero Quest
Given that this mythic foundation is so prevalent in literature, let's travel with Holden Caulfield, the hero of the classic novel *The Catcher in the Rye,* as he takes us on a guided tour along the six-step path that Campbell defines as the Hero Quest.

### I. The hero is called to action
At the beginning of *The Catcher in the Rye,* Holden Caulfield has just been kicked out of prep school. Confused and disillusioned, he sets out on his search for self amidst the noise and clamor of a confusing world.

### 2. An irresistible force impels the hero to accept the call
Propelled by the experience of the death of his younger brother and his craving to find meaning in a world of "phonies," Holden fights with his roommate and then, eager to escape, leaves prep school and begins his journey home to New York City.

### 3. The hero crosses into the Underworld

Holden takes the train to New York. But not wanting to break the news to his parents that he's been kicked out of yet another school, he doesn't go home immediately. Instead Holden checks into a hotel and waits until his mom and dad have received the official letter from the school headmaster informing them of the latest bad news about their son.

Confused and in search of a way to save himself, Holden arranges a series of encounters with people ranging from a cab driver to a prostitute to an old girlfriend. But all of the experiences turn out badly, leaving Holden even more adrift and alone in a dark and alien world.

### 4. The hero confronts the greatest danger and achieves the ultimate truth

Depressed and lonely, Holden wanders the streets of the city. There he meets several people from his past. But nobody can anchor him to a sense of his own reality. Desperate, Holden sneaks into his house and wakes up his younger sister, Phoebe.

In a poignant conversation steeped in the pain of lost innocence, Phoebe asks Holden what he wants to be. He wants to be a catcher in the rye, Holden tells her. He wants to stand guard over little children as they play in a field of rye; to stand at the edge of a cliff and save the children before they fall. This one act would give his life purpose and meaning. But it is, of course, a fantasy. Ultimately, Holden realizes that it is his sister that he must catch. But in the fisherman's parlance, toward the end of the story, he finally understands that the only way he can save Phoebe is with an attitude of "catch and release."

### 5. The hero is unsure he can leave the Underworld

Confused—not knowing where to go or what to do—Holden continues to wander the city. Then he arranges to meet Phoebe in Central Park. In a last nod to his dying innocence, Holden buys a ticket for his sister to ride on the carousel. Later, he says he's going to run away. But in his fragile emotional state, this seems unlikely.

## 6. The hero decides to return to the Upper World, but is changed forever and cannot return to where he began

At the end of the story, Holden informs the reader that he ultimately returned home to his parents' house. He refuses to explain why, but it is implied that he understood that the only way out of his psychic pain was to travel through the long dark night—in a psychiatric facility, it turns out—until he reached the other side. While in the hospital, he talks about trying a new school and about missing the people he used to know. At the very end of the story, Holden understands he will once again enter the world—his innocence lost, but his desire to begin a new life intact.

This, then, is the Hero Quest: the journey from innocence to understanding. The search for meaning and the longing for home. The passing through darkness on the way to the light.

As you write your story, conceive of your hero as going on his or her own quest. Whether you're creating a romance or a science-fiction novel, you can use these six stages defined by Campbell as the guide for your hero and the structure for your tale. If you do this, your narrative will be anchored in character and your plot will support your story.

# PLOT

Plot is nothing more than the way you organize your story—the way you fit the puzzle pieces together to form a connected and coherent picture for the reader. Whether you use Greek Drama, the Hero Quest, action and reaction, or the basic rules of beginning, middle, and end, plot is the glue that holds character and story together and that makes the story compelling to read.

## Ten Principles of a Strong Plot

**1. Choose one idea, a few characters, and a few incidents.** Don't overburden your story with too many plot lines, obstacles, and distractions. If you have a strong character, you can create a textured and complex story within the structure of a simple plot by creating compelling situations—physical or emotional—for your hero to experience.

**2. Create a defining conflict.** At the beginning of the book, make certain the reader understands what the central conflict of the narrative is. This sets up the story for all the action that follows.

**3. Practice tough love.** Just because you write a scene, you don't have to include it in the book. If a scene doesn't advance the plot or develop the characters, rewrite it or get rid of it. Remember that cut scenes are never a waste of time. They're simply prep work on the road to a strong story.

**4. Use action to translate character into plot.** When the hero confronts an obstacle, the action that follows is a result of the hero's response to the obstacle. Reaction follows action. New action follows reaction. The oppositional series of actions drives the character's behavior and evokes the responses that define that character.

**5. Remember that choice creates conflict and pain.** Without choice, there is no conflict. In literature, as in life, the torment of deciding between two equally weighted alternatives creates one of the most powerful conflicts a character can confront. As John Gardner's Grendel says in a devastating summation of life, "Things fade. Alternatives exclude."

**6. Use obstacles to pull story from beginning to end.** Moving from one obstacle to the next creates steady forward momentum and helps maintain a strong story line.

**7. Write with a consciousness of pacing and tension.** In the rising action of your story, you can maintain reader interest by upping the action ante with each succeeding scene. The initial obstacle the hero overcomes should be smaller than the one that follows.

**8. Create suspense by setting limits.** *Limit time:* If the hero must accomplish his goal by a certain time, day, or date, the motivation for continuing to read is automatically built into the story. Will the hero succeed in time, or won't he?

*Limit revelations:* Parcel out pieces of the plot puzzle one item at a time. And parcel out resolutions to the dilemma one detail at a time. Nothing should be solved all at once. If you answer all your questions in one scene, there's nothing left to tell and the story is over. And if you try to wait until the end to resolve all the standing conflicts, chances are readers will get bored with your book long before they make it to the big payoff. The rhythm with which you answer questions and offer resolutions affects the pacing of your story; this is the difference between a slow read and a page-turner.

**9. Remember that action springs from character.** The way you keep your story compelling and your plot honest is to make certain that whatever your hero does, it comes out of an authentic place. Just as shy people don't walk into a room full of strangers without fear, it's important to remember that the hero's character dictates the response to the action. Action does not dictate character.

**10. Dramatize the resolution.** As I emphasized in the section on endings, be sure to play out your ending in full and on stage. Anything less cheats the reader.

## SUBPLOT

A subplot is a smaller story arc nested within the larger narrative. Its path can intersect with the larger plot, run parallel to the plot, or stand in opposition to it. Think of it as a story told in a quieter voice than the plot; it's not meant to upstage the hero's journey but to add texture, interest, and meaning to it. As storytelling devices, subplots supplement, enlighten, and enlarge ... and they provide a way to add interest, increase suspense, and enrich your story.

Some stories have one subplot. Some have several. The choice is up to you. Most novels have several subplots. On the other hand, short stories might have one or none. The choice of how many depends on the complexity of your story. Like Goldilocks, you'll probably have to sample the metaphorical porridge or chair or bed before you find the plot elements that are "just right."

As a general rule, try to envision your story as a tale that includes both plot and subplot. This allows you to expand the narrative horizons, enrich the texture, and increase the depth of both your action and your characters.

## TRICKS OF THE TRADE
### Subplot Characters: The Weight and Scene Rule

Be sure to give your protagonist the most weight and the most scenes in the story. Never forget that the hero is the important character, the one to whom the preponderance of attention must be paid. The secondary character should never share equal time or prominence with the protagonist. This confuses the reader and leads her astray. It also dilutes the distinction of the hero.

This means that, no matter how interesting the subplot is, the secondary character should never get as many scenes as the protagonist. If you violate this rule, you risk losing the reader's allegiance to the hero. There's no precise formula for the scene count, but there shouldn't be any question in the reader's mind about which character dominates the story.

## Six Strategies for Subplot

Subplots enhance your story in several different ways. Don't be afraid to experiment with unusual approaches. Keep trying until you find the method that feels right for both your plot and your characters.

### I. Create a subplot that pulls the reader through the story

In *Wuthering Heights,* Emily Brontë drives the plot through the use of flashbacks that involve two separate narrators: Mr. Lockwood, who is renting a house in Yorkshire from the brooding Heathcliff; and Nelly Dean, the housekeeper at Wuthering Heights, the estate where Heathcliff lives.

After numerous deaths, alliances, vendettas, unions, marriages, and births, the two separate plots—grounded in past and present—come together in an explosive yet muted finish. The backstories, beginning thirty years earlier, drive and shape the current story—that of the mysterious, brooding Heathcliff and what happened to him as a young man and what happens to him as he nears the end of his life. Only through the subplot from the past does the story of what is happening in the present come into focus.

Brontë understood that past illuminates present. And she accomplished her goal with consummate skill.

## 2. Alternate plot and subplot

Jennifer Eagan's layered gothic mystery, *The Keep,* is narrated by an imprisoned convict named Ray who is desperate to connect with his writing teacher, Geneva Carr. His current situation—his need to escape his cell along with his growing connection to Ms. Carr—alternates with the story he writes about two cousins, Danny and Howie. In Ray's fictional story, the two men travel to a castle hidden somewhere in Eastern Europe where they re-enact a prank from childhood that culminates in a more catastrophic finish than before.

The castle is haunted—or not. And the men are allies—or not.

In the novel, the prisoner's story and the cousins' story alternate, moving the action toward an explosive climax that brings the crimes of past and present together.

## 3. Weave plot and subplot together

In *To Kill a Mockingbird,* Harper Lee seamlessly blends her two plots. The first involves Atticus Finch, the single father of two children, defending a black man on trial for raping a white woman. The second is the story of the children hoping to discover the secrets of their mysterious neighbor, Boo Radley. In this unforgettable tale, there is never a moment when the separate stories become confused. And whether you're watching the movie or reading the novel, there is never a moment in which the plot doesn't move smoothly from one scene to the next.

Here, the weaving of plot (the trial of a black man falsely accused of rape) and subplot (the children's interactions with, and "investigations" of, Boo Radley) is carried off with consummate skill. Toward the end of the book, the two plot lines come together when the children encounter a man so angry at their father for exposing his lies in court that he assaults the innocents. It is the mysterious and scary Boo Radley who saves their lives, bringing both stories to completion in this electrifying denouement.

## 4. Use the subplot for comic or romantic relief

William Shakespeare was a master of using the subplot for comic relief. Nowhere is this better portrayed than in *A Midsummer Night's Dream*.

The midsummer story begins with the wedding plans of Theseus, Duke of Athens, and Hippolyta, the Amazon queen. But the plot focuses on Hermia, who has been promised to Demetrius, but who is in love with Lysander. The two young lovers escape together into the forest, pursued by Demetrius and Helena, the woman who loves him.

In the subplot, Oberon and Titania, the king and queen of the fairies, are having an argument about the destiny of a young Indian prince the couple is raising. In an effort to best Titania, Oberon commissions Puck, the merry prankster, to sprinkle love potion in the eyes of the fairy queen and Demetrius, whom the king overheard being cruel to Helena. When Puck mistakes Lysander for Demetrius, the pairs of lovers become even more star-crossed. This entertaining, amusing subplot of trickery and intrigue lends comedy and romance to the story and ultimately brings about the changes that unite the lovers who truly belong together.

## 5. Use the subplot to reveal the character of the hero

In *Anna Karenina,* Leo Tolstoy uses multiple subplots to elicit reactions and responses from Anna Karenina, a woman locked in a painful marriage to Alexei Alexandrovich Karenin while in love with the dashing Count Vronsky.

The novel is awash in subplots of alliances made and broken, of loves found and lost or merely tossed away. And in the midst of this personal and social chaos, Anna summons the strength to break the rules. She leaves her husband and, for all intents and purposes, abandons her child. Her misfortune is that she cannot cope with the consequences of her actions—which are tragic and substantial. Friends and family try to intervene on her behalf. But Anna's ultimate inability to respond with strength to the adverse circumstances of her life exposes her weakness of character and, in the end, drives her to suicide.

## 6. Dramatize the subplot as a story within a story

There's story within a story. Then there's story within a story within a story. From Sanskrit literature through *The Odyssey* and all the way up to *The Itchy and Scratchy Show* in *The Simpsons,* this is a time-honored storytelling device.

In Edgar Allen Poe's *The Fall of the House of Usher,* the narrator of the story comes to the home of his old friend Roderick Usher, who has summoned him because he is ill. Usher is in the midst of a psychological crisis. He believes that his house is sentient—that it knows things.

Soon after the narrator's arrival, Usher informs him that his sister has died and he wants to inter her in the family vault below the house for two weeks before she is buried.

To distract his friend from his misery, the narrator begins to read a book to Usher called *The Mad Trist.* The problem is, the action that happens in the book begins to take place in the House of Usher. This parallel haunting drives Usher over the brink as he confesses that his sister isn't really dead and that he fears she is behind the door. She is indeed there, having clawed her way out of her tomb. And after she accomplishes this feat, she collapses on Usher and they both die.

Hence, the story within the story affects the "real" story. Mirrored storytelling is challenging, but it's a plot technique that can be effective when used with skill.

# CREATING AN OUTLINE
# FOR ESTABLISHING PLOT LINES

1. Think of your story as divided into three acts:

- Act I: Problem/obstacle
- Act II: Conflict/struggle
- Act III: Resolution

Outline the central action in each act. Then ask yourself how the hero's story can be adjusted to honor the idea of the Hero Quest.

2. Once your plot trajectory is clear, add a subplot. To brainstorm possible subplots, consider the following: What secondary character's question, problem, or struggle would strengthen or illuminate an element of your main plot? What outside forces might work to reveal the hero's character?

3. Next, decide whether you are going to weave the subplot into the plot, present it in alternating stories with the plot, or devise some combination of those two techniques.

4. Finally, as you write, refer to the guidelines I've offered for story, plot, and subplot, remembering that even as these suggestions make demands, they also shape and strengthen story.

*Cleene* 13 *∽elle*

# THE CAST OF CHARACTERS
## The Good, the Bad, and the Ugly

---

*A writer can never know about a*
*character's feelings what is not somewhere*
*mirrored in her own.*

—Katherine Paterson

How your characters act and react—how they think and feel; how they handle obstacles and respond to people, places, and things—*is* story.

If you create a static character, no matter how riveting your action is, your story will fall flat. Your challenge as a writer is to create a character that lives and breathes on the page, a character that laughs and cries and makes the reader feel those emotions.

When I reflect on the characters I treasured when I was young, I think about Nancy Drew and Holden Caulfield. Nancy was brave and daring—everything I wasn't but wanted to be. And Holden ... Holden was anguished and confused—everything I was but wanted not to be. Both of these characters not only evoked powerful feelings in me, they are permanently engraved in my memory. They also mark a distinctive footprint in the literary sand for generations of writers.

## FIRST IMPRESSIONS

Psychologist Eugene T. Gendlin talks about a "felt sense" we can learn to acknowledge and access when we encounter a specific experience. This is analogous to the visceral response we feel when we first meet a character on the screen or on the pages of a book. Sissy Hankshaw in *Even Cowgirls Get the Blues* and Easy Rawlins in *Devil in a Blue Dress* summon totally different sensibilities in the reader. Yet the characters have one significant quality in common: From the moment you meet them, they jump off the page and take up permanent residence in your imagination.

It's said about people that the first impression is the lasting impression. That applies to fiction, too. As far as stories are concerned, this doesn't mean the initial introduction to the main character should be an elaborate happening. Nor does it need to be a whiz-bang, five-star event. But it does mean the introduction should be memorable.

Sometimes the quietest beginning can establish a character in the reader's mind. In *Katherine*, Anya Seton introduces her titular character in a subdued but memorable fashion.

> In the tender green time of April, Katherine set forth at last upon her journey with the two nuns and the royal messenger.
>
> The invisible sun had scarcely risen as they quitted the little convent of Sheppey, and guiding the horses westward towards the Kentish mainland, rode gingerly down the steep hill. Dripping dun clouds obscured the minster tower behind them and thick mists blew in from the North Sea.
>
> The bell began tolling for Prime and Katherine heard, through its familiar clangor, the bang of the

> priory's gate and the faint voice of the little wicket
> nun calling again through the mist, "Adieu, dear Kath-
> erine, adieu."

There's nothing flashy here. Nothing audacious. But there is something deeply evocative—almost elegiac—about this simple introduction. We feel Katherine's dignity and we sense that she must bear some sort of resemblance to the land through which she walks. We also sense this is a character we want to invite into our imagination.

At the opposite end of the spectrum, I return to Holden Caulfield, from J.D. Salinger's *The Catcher in the Rye*:

> If you really want to hear about it, the first thing you'll
> probably want to know is where I was born, and what
> my lousy childhood was like, and how my parents were
> occupied and all before they had me, and all that David
> Copperfield kind of crap, but I don't feel like going into
> it, if you want to know the truth.

Which of us didn't feel alienated when we were teenagers? And which of us didn't draw comfort from reading about an adolescent who reflected the feelings—if not the circumstances—that overwhelmed us from time to time?

Salinger captures Holden in one powerful introductory sentence. Lurking beneath the angst there's just a whiff of humor. Maybe it's the use of a word like *lousy*. Or maybe it's the nakedness of the hero's angst. But I have never known a reader who wasn't mesmerized by the protagonist of this brilliantly realized novel.

From Captain Ahab to Yossarian to Easy Rawlins, from Jay Gatsby to Don Corleone to Precious Ramotswe, the characters who capture the hearts and minds of readers are the characters whose lives are fully realized in the imaginations of the writer. Your most fundamental challenge, then, is to know the person you're writing about. If you understand the character, both inside and out, you will create someone people want to read about.

# LASTING IMPRESSIONS

When you approach your characters, remember it is not only the hero who must stand out. All the characters in your story—major and minor characters—should occupy a unique place in your own imagination in order for them to occupy that same status in the reader's imagination.

## A Matter of Authenticity

Before you become too involved in writing your story, take the time to do everything you can to establish the essence of your character in your own mind.

A strong character doesn't behave the way you want him to. A strong character behaves the way he should. Every time you write a new scene ask yourself if your hero's action is authentic.

If you're writing about a woman who is excruciatingly shy, she can't walk into a party where she doesn't know anyone and introduce herself to the nearest stranger. Not going to happen. A shy woman can't do this unless she's been preparing for this bold step for months.

Almost nothing yanks readers out of a story faster than when they feel a character's actions are inauthentic. If readers can't believe in or don't understand your hero, they have absolutely no reason to invest in your story. That doesn't mean they must share similar lives. But it does mean that they must share common feelings. Keep in mind that the actions of the character must be organic; they must grow naturally from the heart and mind of that character. Once you've established this foundation, you can move forward into your story with confidence.

# THE FUNDAMENTALS OF CHARACTER

Readers like to identify with the characters they are reading about. If your reader can't empathize with the character in some way, you risk losing your audience. You don't establish this connection by trying to mirror the average experience of the average reader. You establish this connection by telling us what is unique about the character and plunging her into a specific situation.

In Diablo Cody's coming-of-age movie *Juno*—about a sixteen-year-old girl's surprise pregnancy—the character is drawn with such wit, insight, and skill that the viewer cheers for her from the opening scene to the final credits.

Juno is a brave, scared, sassy, defensive, smart, vulnerable, assertive teenager who isn't afraid to be herself. She is, as her boyfriend's mother brands her, "different." And she summons the courage to do what she must to survive.

Here, the age of the viewer doesn't matter. Approximately one eon separates me from a sixteen-year-old girl (praise the Lord). But I remember those years. At that age, I was too scared to be impudent, too eager to fit in, and too insecure to be different. In fact, there is little that my teenage self and Juno have in common. But that didn't keep me from becoming engrossed in the movie and rooting for the survival of this teen who is, in fact, a soul sister of Holden Caulfield—as memorable in her voice and perspective, and as universal in her vulnerability.

With that scenario in mind, your hero can live in the desert, rescue stray dogs, be an alien, or pan for gold in the Yukon. It doesn't matter where the hero lives or what he does. As long as the emotions and responses of the character are authentic, the reader can still create a bond with him.

There isn't a person alive who hasn't, at one time or another, felt like an alien. There's not a person alive who hasn't been embarrassed in front of his peers, disappointed in the face of hope, or embroiled in conflicts with friends. The themes are familiar and the feelings these circumstances evoke are universal. No matter where they take place or under what circumstances they are played out, readers can relate to them.

## HOW TO CREATE UNIQUE CHARACTERS

It's easy to write about common emotions. Anger, sadness, and joy are familiar and accessible to any reader. Make every effort to dig deeper when you envision people you want to write about.

We don't live in a black-and-white world. Neither should our characters. Paint your characters in both bright and muted shades. Look for conflicts. Look for subtleties. No need to hammer on a point. Readers are smart enough to pick up on your clues.

## Validate Confusion

Seek out the confusion in the feelings of your character, the unconscious emotions that drive a person to behave in one way or another.

One of the easiest ways to do this is to create a character who faces a bewildering, equally weighted choice. Because choice not only creates agony, it eliminates possibility.

Choosing defines who we are and generates consequences we're destined to carry throughout our lives. At its extreme, the choice is life and death, a situation William Styron carried to the most excruciating limit in *Sophie's Choice*. In the novel, Sophie Zawistowska arrives at Auschwitz with her two children, a son and a daughter. At the point of entry, a sadistic doctor forces her to choose which child will go to the gas chamber and which child will go to the concentration camp. Life or death, no going back. And there's no forgetting that scene. *Ever.* Watching her child walk toward certain death because of a choice she made brands Sophie's soul forever. The guilt from that one moment impacts her dark, anguished and self-destructive behavior throughout the story. And in the end it also drives her to suicide.

## Honor Emotions

In all your characters, it's critical to honor the emotional underpinnings that support and drive their behavior. This isn't just because the character should behave in a believable way. It's because a reader's emotions must tie into the character's emotions if you want to create a memorable story.

In *Gone With the Wind*, who would Scarlett O'Hara be without passion backed up by a will of iron? Like the collective psyche of the antebellum South, she is spoiled, she is vain, and she is selfish. So why should we care? Because she is a woman who will *not* be defeated. She does what she must do to save herself, her family, and her beloved Tara. And she does it with a passion so fiery, so invested in outcome that we cheer for her success in spite of her glaring flaws.

How did Margaret Mitchell accomplish this? By creating emotions that match the drama of the story measure for measure. Furthermore, the conflicts playing out in Scarlett—her ambivalence about the men in her life, her fierce determination to overcome any obstacle and pay any price—enlist the reader's sympathies.

In fact, how can you *not* cheer for a woman who shakes her fist at the fates and declares, "As God is my witness ... the Yankees aren't going to lick me. ... If I have to steal or kill—as God is my witness, I'm never going to be hungry again."

When we read this book, Scarlett's emotions become our emotions. And because of that, we support her from the opening line to *Frankly, my dear, I don't give a damn.*

## Celebrate Inconsistency

Contradictions make characters more interesting. This applies to heroes as well as to villains. No one is entirely consistent in thoughts, feelings, or behavior. As much as I'd like to have you believe that I'm a woman with a great memory, a loving nature, and a generous spirit, if you paint me into a corner, I'll cop to the fact that I'm also a woman with a lousy memory, a reclusive nature, and a cranky spirit.

So, instead of ignoring the contradictions in characters, use them to your advantage. It is, after all, the intrigue of opposites that makes a character interesting.

For instance, when analyzing the historical character of T.E. Lawrence—the man on whom the film of *Lawrence of Arabia* was modeled—Lowell Thomas talked about how Lawrence worked hard to maintain his privacy after his return to England from fighting in the Arab Revolt during World War I. He even went so far as to live under assumed names. And yet, Thomas says, this extraordinary man "had a genius for backing into the limelight."

In David Lean's movie, the dashing British Lieutenant, played by the dashing Peter O'Toole, is repulsed by violence ... and yet he is also drawn to it. He's depicted as a tormented man who shuns war, but once he is involved in the revolt, he becomes a strategic and ruthless warrior, willing to do anything to achieve victory.

It's no wonder that this historical character was a natural for transformation into an epic film. Lawrence is handsome; he is shy. He is fierce; he is tender. He is brutal and he is remorseful. It's the contradiction, not the consistency, that makes his character one of the most memorable in film history.

## Ignore the Facts

Lots of us have written about characters who mirror people we know in real life. Depending on what kind of person inspires you, this process can either be enlightening or inhibiting. If we're intent on reflecting the reality of someone we know, there are two primary issues to keep in mind.

### 1. Ignore the opinions of others

Often when writers create a character, they are inhibited by the fear of what the real-life person that the character is based on—or those people who read the book—will think about what they have written. It would be foolhardy to create an exact duplicate of someone you know. But you should not be inhibited by what others might think or say. The writer's craft is full of risk. Creating characters is one of them. As Anne Lamott once said, "Write as if your parents are dead."

### 2. Ignore the truth

As I mentioned in chapter twelve on creating plot, learn to ignore reality in order to find the deeper truth. This means you might have to discard or transform what you know. Just because the person on whom you're modeling your character wouldn't say or do something, this doesn't mean your fictional character wouldn't say or do it.

## TRICKS OF THE TRADE
### Choose Your Names Carefully

Names are important. They're not something to be considered lightly. Sometimes you might want the name you choose for your character to reflect who she is. Other times you can go for contrast and the name can reflect who she is not. A regular, average, well-behaved kid can be Jane or she can be Seraphina. A nasty little bully can be named Buck or Ralphie. Each evokes a different response in the reader.

I recently edited a book in which four characters had names that began with J. Two of them were quite similar. In the beginning, I had trouble telling the characters apart. Was it Julie who made the secret phone call? Or was it Judy?

When readers first approach a story, one of their primary needs is to remember "which one is which." Your task is to help them out. With this in mind, make the effort to give your characters names that can be easily distinguished. The easiest way to do this is have each name start with a different letter of the alphabet. Lina and Lillie aren't as easy to differentiate and remember as Lina and Allison.

# QUESTIONS OF CHARACTER

Creating a sense of wholeness and complexity in your character goes beyond knowing where she comes from, how many siblings she has, and where she lives and goes to school. Character is made up of endless aspects of circumstances, influences, locations, feelings, thoughts, conflicts, and preferences. This does not mean you have to demonstrate all these things. But it does mean you should be aware of the multiple facets of your character as you write.

## A Brainstorming List for Creating Characters

There are endless ways to flesh out a character. One way to create multiple dimensions in a person who inhabits the pages of your book is to imagine different aspects of that character's inner and outer life. Here's a list of possible character traits for you to consider. This is a taking-off point—a framework to help you invent fully rounded and interesting characters. Add to it. Subtract from it. Embellish, embroider, and expand it. But most of all, use it.

- **Personality:** Is your character aggressive or passive? Brave or fearful? Confident or shy? Creative? Eccentric? Introverted or extroverted? Logical? Optimistic or pessimistic? Paranoid? Risk-averse or risk-taking?

- **Defining traits:** Could your character be described as a bully or an underdog? A geek or a loner? A joiner or a leader? On the other hand, is he cold *and* warm? Confrontational *and* eager to please? Defiant *and* indifferent? Disliked? Feared? The life of the party or reclusive?

- **Origin:** Did your character grow up in an urban or rural area? In the big city or a small town? On which continent? In which country? With one parent or both? Was he an orphan? (How do these things affect his worldview?)

- **Home:** Where does your character hang his hat? In a city or the suburbs? On the coast or in the plains? On an island? In the mountains? In the desert?

- **Shelter:** In what kind of building does your character live? Apartment? Farm? House? What architecture style? Mansion? Public housing? Ranch? Shack? On the street?

- **Family constellation:** Does your character have children or grandchildren? Are her grandparents still living?

Is she single, married, separated, or divorced? What's her relationship with her parent(s) or stepparent(s)? Where does she fall in the birth order? Does she have any pets?

- **Best friends:** Who are your character's best friends? What genders are they? How did they meet? What's the nature of the relationships? What interests do they share? How often do they communicate with one another?

- **Interests:** What is your character passionate about? Art, music, film, literature? Animals? The environment? Science and technology? Politics and religion? Culture, cuisine, and travel? Sports and games?

- **Dislikes:** What repulses or irritates your character? Leafy green vegetables? Classical music? The opposite sex? Rude drivers?

- **Favorites:** What's your character's favorite ... artist? Book or author? Clothing line? Color? Song? Flower? Food? Game? Sport? Movie or TV show?

- **Hobbies:** When your character isn't at work, she's spending her time ... antiquing? Camping? Coin or stamp collecting? Gaming? Gardening? Cooking? Painting, drawing, or sculpting? Parachute jumping or rock climbing? Shopping? Volunteering?

- **Clothes:** How does your character dress—casual, trendy, sloppy, formal? Does he take pride in his appearance? Does he spend money on clothes?

- **Names:** Does your character have a nickname? If so, what does that name reflect—her appearance, circumstance, personality? Does she like or hate her nickname? If she's married, did she take her spouse's name?

- **Body language:** How does your character carry himself? Does he stand straight? Make eye contact? Have a limp handshake? Walk as if defeated—with slumped shoulders? Glide gracefully down hallways? Trip and fall often?

As you apply these particulars, preferences, and circumstances to your character, ask yourself the following questions:

- Is my character too bland? Too homogenous?
- How do the traits reflect the heart and spirit of my character?
- How do they demonstrate who he is and what he stands for?
- How do these traits indicate emotional conflict?
- What do they say about his inner life?
- What do they say about his outer life?
- How do the traits indicate the complexity of the character?
- What other traits, circumstances, or preferences can add depth and texture and conflicts to the character?

## TIPS FOR CREATING MEMORABLE CHARACTERS

Once you've settled on these primary manifestations, it's time to consider some of the finer points of creating a noteworthy fictional personality—a personality that can be a major or a minor character.

### State What the Character Wants

In the beginning, the character must state what he wants and spend the rest of the story trying to get it. This can be done either explicitly or implicitly. In *Ordinary Heroes*, Scott Turow opens his first chapter with this line:

> All parents keep secrets from their children. My father, it seemed, kept more than most.

Without addressing his quest directly, in just two sentences, the first-person narrator enlists the reader's allegiance by asking us to take on the hero's task to discover the truth about his father. In fact, the entire novel is built on the investigation of what exactly happened to his father in World War II, why he had been court-martialed, and if his actions might redeem his honor.

## Honor the Struggle

In the section on dead ends in chapter ten, I talked about the book I edited in which the hero started out lying to his parents and he ended doing the same thing. The character had not increased his understanding, broadened his knowledge, or expanded his self-awareness. From start to finish, he had neither grown nor changed.

Prolonged observation of the status quo is slightly less interesting than watching grass grow. It is the struggle—not the satisfaction—that makes us root for a character and makes a story worth reading. In order to do this, you must begin at a place in the story that leaves the hero room to grapple with his problem.

In Anne Rice's *Interview With the Vampire*, the year is 1791 and a young plantation owner named Louis is transformed into an immortal one by the bite of the vampire Lestat. Lestat has no trouble at all feasting off the blood of the plantation slaves—or anyone else, for that matter. But in two hundred years of wandering the world, Louis continues to be tormented by the pain he inflicts on others. Beyond this immediate problem, he eventually comes to detest the suffering that immortality represents.

Louis's struggle between morality and survival is epic. And in that struggle, Rice creates nuanced characters that are touching and flawed and memorable.

## Add Conflict

Conflict creates drama and defines character. Without conflict, plot does not exist, you have no story, and your character has nothing to overcome. Toss your character in the midst of one of the four fundamental conflicts described in chapter twelve:

1. Man against man
2. Man against nature
3. Man against society
4. Man against self

## Portray Vivid Personalities

This task is easier said than done. Part of the secret of creating dynamic personalities is to make characters courageous in their confrontation with their demons and determined in their drive to overcome the obstacles they encounter. This does not mean they are fearless. But it does mean they must overcome their fear in order to step up to the plate and be counted.

When it comes to vivid personalities, think of Emma, Oliver Twist, Ahab, Sissy Hankshaw, Huckleberry Finn, Yossarian, Hannibal Lecter, Captain Queeg, Holly Golightly, and Don Corleone. They may be good or they may be evil, but they are all painted in blazing colors. Along with definite opinions and strong spirits, they have quirks, both good and bad, that set them apart from others around them.

## Create Convincing Motivation

Authenticity—of thought, behavior, and action—is what makes a character come alive on the page. This concept can be honored in a complex tale about the clash between good and evil or in the simplest book written for children.

Pat Conroy creates a convincing motivation for his character, Tom Wingo, in *The Prince of Tides*. Here, the hero is called to New York to help rescue his twin sister from psychological hell. He has no idea that in order to accomplish this goal, he will have to enter into his own personal underworld. His quest to uncover old secrets, heal new wounds, and save his sister motivates his character from the first page to the last.

## Reflect Unspoken Feelings in Someone or Something Else

There's a reason why "It was a dark and stormy night" has taken on a life of its own. In spite of the jokes about this clichéd opening, the weather often stands as a reflection of the mood of a book or the feelings of a character. Beyond hurricanes and sunny days, reflecting a character's feelings in another being is a powerful way to convey the inner reality of a character.

On a grand scale, Herman Melville sets up Moby-Dick, the mythical and elusive white whale, as the reflection of Captain

Ahab's obsession and the embodiment of his demons. Ahab is a driven man with only one goal: revenge against the whale that caused him to lose his leg. Nothing else matters—not his religion, not his ship, not the lives of his crew.

Here, the mighty whale embodies the destructive power of obsession—its selfishness and virulence and the carnage it creates—culminating in a scene in which Ahab becomes entangled in the rope of the harpoon with which he spears the whale. He's hoisted on his own petard, both metaphorically and, for all intents and purposes, physically. In the end, wounded monster and wounded master disappear into the deep, taking the ship and its crew with them. There is only one survivor to tell the tale: Ishmael, of "Call me Ishmael" fame.

*The Horse Whisperer*—a novel by Nicholas Evans and a movie starring Robert Redford—tells the story of Grace, who is injured in a horrible accident in which she and her horse, Pilgrim, are hit by a truck. Both human and animal are traumatized, inwardly and outwardly, by the event. And each reflects the other's pain.

When Grace plunges into a deep depression and all seems hopeless, Grace's mother hires Tom Booker to heal the horse. But this handsome, dashing horse whisperer realizes he cannot accomplish this goal without healing the owner, too. Thus, human and animal reflect each other's pain and progress.

Whether it's joy or anxiety or sadness, search for new ways to show the reader what the hero feels. You will be rewarded with a more intriguing portrait for your efforts and a more enthusiastic audience for your story.

## Present Multi-faceted Villains

When most people think of a villain, they think of a thoroughly bad guy. But a singularly dark and nefarious character isn't half as intriguing as a conflicted villain. As I said before, people are not consistent. And an all-bad-all-the-time villain is a boring villain.

In *The Godfather*, Mario Puzo created a villain for the ages. As a young man, Vito Corleone was smuggled to America to avoid being killed by an enemy of his father's. He later became a ruthless mob boss for whom extortion was child's play and honor killing was *de rigueur*. Yet, in his own way, the Godfather was a kind and generous man who lived by a strict moral code that embraced family values and eschewed hard drugs.

These conflicting modes of behavior made Corleone a fascinating villain—a much more memorable one than if he had simply been an all-around bad guy.

## Create Empathetic Situations

The easiest way to enlist a reader's empathy is to create situations the reader can relate to. Embarrassment, joy, loneliness, longing, fear, happiness, relief, insecurity, anticipation, anxiety—all are universal expressions of the human condition. These feelings tap into the deepest part of a reader's psyche, inviting her to join the hero in sharing the emotions common to us all.

In his remarkable novel *A Separate Peace*, John Knowles explores the complexities associated with the demands of friendship, the intrusion of evil, and the limits of loyalty in a boy's boarding school. Phineas is the golden boy, the daredevil, the handsome, dazzling athlete all the other students envy: "He possessed an extra vigor, a heightened confidence in himself, a serene capacity for affection which saved him."

Gene is the narrator of the story who looks back on a fateful summer he spent at school as an insecure, lonely, introverted teen. He admired his friend Phineas for breaking the rules. But he also envied him and ultimately tried to live through him. The pivotal point in Gene's youth is when he and Phineas attended summer session in order to earn their high school diplomas before they were drafted to fight in World War II.

One afternoon, Gene and Phineas go down to the river where they prepare to jump off a tree limb together and dive into the water below. Without consciousness of his own jealousy, Gene joggles the limb, causing Phineas to fall onto the ground and break his leg. Afterward, Gene is overcome with guilt and confesses his act to his friend. But Phineas can't accept the explanation. He's one of those rare innocents who believes in the innate goodness of people, and it's impossible for him to consider that his friend might have harmed him on purpose. It was an accident, that's all.

In this quietly powerful novel, Knowles explores the complexity of feelings—jealousy, identity, redemption—associated with the bonds of friendship and the cruelty of adolescents. He also examines the corrosion of envy and indifference of evil.

And Knowles accomplishes this fictional feat by offering Gene's elegiac examination of the past and how it intrudes on—and corrodes—his life. Here, the author invites the reader to experience the full range of emotions—not just read about them—that are presented in the story. It's no wonder this book has been in print for nearly fifty years.

## Make Certain the Hero Saves Himself

A couple of years ago, I edited a book about a young man who struggles to escape the tyranny of his stepfather. At the end of the story when it appears as if the hero will never be able to stand up to this bully, his best buddy steps in and calls the police, exposing all the stepfather's evil doings. A happy ending? Yes. But how has the young man grown? He hasn't. What did he learn? Nothing. Where is the gratification for the reader? There isn't any.

This kind of nonconfrontational denouement might technically constitute a happy ending. But it's also a boring ending. Let me remind you that this is art, not life. The fact is, as well intentioned as this solution might be, the reader won't find satisfaction in the storytelling unless the hero learns to defend himself and confront his nemesis. Furthermore, this scene must be dramatized "on stage" for the reader, not presented as one character telling another about the confrontation.

In *Harry Potter and the Deathly Hallows*—the last book of the Harry Potter series—the young hero reaches the point where he must confront his lifelong nemesis, Lord Voldemort. At first, the young lad takes refuge in the castle. But when that fails, he gathers his courage and walks into his enemy's camp in the forest. Voldemort attacks him with the über-powerful Elder Wand, but to no avail. In the end, nobody saves Harry but himself. His courage and magic prevail and the Dark Lord is annihilated.

No matter what kind of story you write or what kind of happy ending you concoct, at the end of the day there is only one rule that applies to this situation: *The hero must be the instrument of his own salvation.* Anything less diminishes the story and cheats the reader.

All of these techniques are essential to creating the intriguing and layered characters who inhabit your books. Each approach can illuminate an aspect of your fictional characters that will allow them to live on the page, as well as in the imaginations of readers.

## EXERCISES IN CHARACTER

1. As you write your own story and create your characters, pay special attention to how you present them to the reader. Then ask yourself the following questions:

- What does the main character want the most?
- What obstacles must the character overcome?
- What makes the character memorable?
- How is the character's inner life revealed?
- How does the hero save herself?

2. Create an in-depth profile of your main character. Then ask yourself the following questions:

- Is the hero authentic?
- Is the hero complex?
- Is the hero conflicted?
- Is the hero convincing?
- Is the hero memorable?
- Is the hero emotionally honest?
- Is the hero's motivation justifiable?
- Is the hero the instrument of his own salvation?

If you can answer yes to all the above questions, chances are you've created a memorable and lasting character.

# 14

# POINT OF VIEW

## Who Tells the Story

---

*[Point of view] isn't only about a character's*
*viewpoint. It's where character meets language,*
*the actual essence of fiction in print.*

—Alicia Rasley

One reason the fiction element of point of view (or POV) creates so much confusion is that the layman's dictionary definition—meaning an opinion, an outlook, an attitude—isn't broad
enough to include the writer's definition. The latter certainly
embraces a narrator's opinions, outlooks, and attitudes. But it
also encompasses a host of critical authorial choices about who
tells the story and how that story is revealed.

In other words, point of view has two parts: The perspective
of a story or character, and the way in which that story or character is expressed. That sounds simple enough. But if you take
a closer look, it soon becomes apparent that you're staring into
the slippery center of a big can of literary worms. Both voice

and theme are tied to the point-of-view discussion (but we'll cover that in chapter seventeen).

Point of view is a complex concept that resists simple explanation (or a standard language to describe it). For instance, what one person calls "neutral omniscient," another person calls the "objective point of view." Then there are the issues of author intrusion vs. subjective viewpoint; point-of-view character vs. focus character; unreliable narrator vs. authoritative narrator vs. implied narrator. Things get more complicated when you collide with shifting point of view, peripheral point of view, panoramic point of view, and omniscient point of view.

Enough already. My personal point of view is that this subject has been unnecessarily complicated by too much critical theory and too little common sense. My goal here is to reaffirm the basics.

## FIRST THINGS FIRST: ONE OR MORE THAN ONE POV?

Before you start writing your story, the first thing you need to do is clarify in your own mind the difference between single and multiple viewpoints.

A tale told from a *single point of view* uses one person's perspective *only*. Everything is filtered through that specific person's eyes, heart, and mind. No other character's thoughts or feelings are directly expressed in the book. This does not mean, however, that you can't show how others feel through their dialogue, their actions, and their reactions to people, places, and events.

In a book with *multiple points of view*, the story is told through the eyes, hearts, and minds of two or more characters. There are times when a narrative demands such a treatment in order to convey the fullness of the story, such as when a romance utilizes both the hero's and heroine's points of view. Then, there's the *omniscient point of view* in which the writer gets to play God and barge into anybody's mind he damn well pleases.

# Who Tells the Story?

To determine the point of view from which you want to write your story, you must ask yourself: Who tells the story?

Lots of different people can tell the same story. Each time the narrator changes, the story changes. The writer's task is to choose the most effective character or characters to tell the tale.

Suppose you're writing a story about Matt almost drowning when he was twenty-five years old. Do you tell the story from his point of view, the point of view of the friend who saved him, or the points of view of Matt's family? Or all of the above? Each of the three approaches would spring from the same set of circumstances, but each would constitute a radically different tale.

## *Matt's POV*

Here, you could tell the story of how Matt trips, hits his head, and falls off of the dock into the water —how helplessness gives way to the monster of panic and how terror soon surrenders to the bliss of departing.

When telling the story this way, you would focus on Matt's emotions, how a fifteen-minute episode transforms his life—not only what he feels at the time of the accident, but also how the experience changes the way he sees himself and the way he relates to other people. Using this point of view creates a more visceral tale, a deeper personal story of how an entire life is colored by one brief episode. It's easier to capture the intense passion of the moment in the first-person point of view.

## *Friend's POV*

It might be intriguing to read about the experience from Matt's friend's point of view—the young woman who pulls Matt out of the water and gives him CPR until the paramedics arrive, the friend who learns what it's like to come close to losing her best friend, and how saving her friend's life changes her own life.

If you want to tell a more exciting, action-packed story, this would be the approach to choose. The tension rises out of calling 911, in taking instructions from the operator about how to perform CPR, in not knowing if the paramedics are going to arrive in time, or if Matt is going to live or die.

### Multiple characters' POV

You could also tell the story about the near-drowning from multiple points of view. Matt can tell the story from his point of view, the friend can tell the story from her point of view, Matt's brother can tell the story from his point of view (colored by his sibling rivalry), and Matt's mother can tell the story from her point of view.

This approach would be more appropriate if you want to tell a human interest story—how one powerful incident changes each person in a different way. The irony here could be that Matt—the person whose life was in jeopardy—is least affected by the incident.

By these examples, you can begin to understand that point of view is about much more than just who's doing the talking. Your choice of narrator also affects the type of story you're telling and how close you allow the reader to experience the intensity of the action. Once you decide *who* tells the story, you can move on to the question of *how* the story is told.

In order to determine how you want to tell your story, it's critical to familiarize yourself with the range of choices available, as well as the advantages and disadvantages of each choice.

## FIRST-PERSON POINT OF VIEW

In a first-person story, the narrator is the *I* of the story. Everything that happens in the book is told from this singular point of view. If you play your cards right, you can hook the reader in the first sentence.

In *Ellen Foster*, Kaye Gibbons begins her novel with this astonishing line: "When I was little I would think of ways to kill my daddy." No muss, no fuss. This opening is shocking, provocative, and compelling. It grabs the reader, yanks her into the head of the narrator, and doesn't let go. Writers new to the craft of storytelling often choose first person because that's how they've written throughout their lives in letters and journals. In fact, that's the voice I chose to write my first novel. I didn't know any other way to write. A caveat, however: It may be comfortable to write from a singular and personal point of view, but it's not always easy.

When you write a story in the first person, your ability to shift from place to place and person to person is limited by the experience of the narrator. Everything you write about must be witnessed by the narrator or told to her by another character. The narrator can only observe and reflect upon those observations; she may not assume anyone thinks or feels anything unless it is manifested in some way. Every scene is written from the first-person narrator's singular point of view; she is our only gateway into the story. Your plot development options are limited when you can't report on anything that takes place out of sight of the narrator.

You also run the risk of sounding repetitive in your writing. Too many *I*s can become tedious. Granted, Caesar did all right when he said, "*Veni, vidi, vici*": "I came, I saw, I conquered." Short, pithy, and to the point. But that approach to writing would get old if he went on and on describing the Gallic Wars in the first person: "I raped, I pillaged, I plundered. I burned, I looted, I spoiled. I sacked, I snatched, I savaged. I robbed, I ravaged, I wept. I crushed, I cried, I gloried. I raided, I captured, I won." That's a lot of interesting action destroyed by a lot of *I*s.

To avoid the *I* trap, structure your sentences carefully so that they don't all begin with the pronoun. Participial phrases are a good way to do this, as in: "Feeling ill at the thought of confronting the man alone, I approached him in the restaurant."

These aren't the only issues to consider, however. Before you decide to write your story in first person, consider the advantages and disadvantages.

## Advantages of First-Person Point of View

- **You create a sense of connection.** The immediacy of first person sets up a direct connection between reader and writer.

- **The reader experiences the intensity of a personal story.** In this point of view, readers have a sense that the story is being told just to them—as if someone is whispering secrets from the pages of a book.

- **You can create an intimate portrait.** Readers feel closer to the action and to the hero. It's easy to slip your imagination into the mind and heart of a first-person narrator.

- **You can create a variety of moods.** You can write in the voice of a tough guy or the voice of a dreamy romantic. It all depends on the story you want to tell and the feelings you want to convey.

## Disadvantages of First-Person Point of View

- **Your story is limited to one point of view.** Since your story cannot expand beyond what the narrator thinks, sees, and hears, no action can take place out of sight of the first-person narrator. The narrator can, however, interpret reactions.

  > Linda looked worried when her mother asked me about the money.

  > Or

  > Dan's voice shook when he told me what happened.

- **Closeness to story can diminish perceptions.** If the point-of-view character is too close to the action, she might not have the perspective to tell an interesting story.

- **Beware of dangerous *Is*.** Too many *Is* can spoil the prose and bore the reader.

# TRICKS OF THE TRADE
## Shifting Location

Although first person is limited to what the narrator sees and thinks, feels and hears, there is a way to move out of sight of the narrator.

If you want to shift to another location, try having the narrator imagine the scene. Let's return to Lia on the ladder from chapter eleven. She knows her lover is waiting for her in the park. But it's a first-person narrative, so we have no choice but to stay right there on those rungs with her. Well ... not exactly. We can shift the action away from Lia and into her imagination with some fictional abracadabra written in the subjunctive voice.

> As I clung to the sides of the ladder, I glanced at my watch. Five minutes after eleven, I thought. I'm already twenty-five minutes late. I could just imagine what Devon was doing.
>
> I could see him pacing back and forth, watching a young couple flirting in the shadows.
>
> My heart sank as I imagined him glancing at his watch and shrugging in that "whatever" kind of way he has when he looks for me to come down the path.
>
> "If she doesn't get here in five minutes, I'm going to leave," he'd mumble. "She won't get a chance to know what real happiness is."
>
> The lovers would giggle, reminding Devon of me.
>
> He'll think I've given up on our love. He'll think I've forsaken him, that I didn't have the courage to risk meeting him. What if he leaves before I get there?

So there you have it: a way to shift "outside" the view of the first-person narrator and still stay within the first-person convention.

Although it requires a little verbal sorcery, shifting the scene by slipping into the projective imagination of the narrator allows you to change the focus to another place or person. At the same time, you can expand the action and create a narrative latitude that strict first person lacks.

So if you want to write in the first person but think it's too limited, try this technique before you reject the possibility. You might find this narrative sleight of hand is all you need to create a well-rounded, single-point-of-view story.

## Unconventional *Is*

If you want to write in first person but the voice feels wrong or you're stuck in the narrative, consider the possibility that the wrong person is telling the story. The narrator does not have to be the protagonist or hero of the story. He can also be a *catalyst*—someone whose ordinary, forgettable act has extraordinary ramifications that create the conflict around which the story is built. The narrator can be an *observer* removed from the protagonist in a significant way—someone who witnesses the action from a distance, perhaps, a brother, a friend, or a classmate. Or the narrator can be a *survivor*—the one who lived to tell the tale the reader is now savoring.

### *The catalyst*

In chemistry, the catalyst is the substance that causes a reaction but itself remains unchanged. Some people are like that. Either accidentally or on purpose, they—or their actions—make things happen.

Consider Alice Sebold's *The Lovely Bones*. The novel opens with the rape, murder, and dismemberment of a fourteen-year-old girl named Susie. After this horrific incident, Susie moves to her own personal heaven, a place from which she is able to watch her grieving family and friends as they deal with the discovery of her body and the aftermath of her death.

Other than being the observer, Susie no longer plays a direct part in the plot. She is merely the observer, the narrator. And yet without her death—the catalyst—there would be no story.

Using an unexpected narrator is an intriguing way to tell a story, one you might consider if the plot and characters lend themselves to such a device.

### The observer's account

Just as in life, sometimes a person can render a more intriguing response to an incident that he witnesses from afar—or that he learns about, rather than experiences. Choosing a narrator that has some distance from the story can give you more leeway to comment on the action of the characters and evaluate their responses to each other. And it can also give you a more surprising perspective on the events that take place.

The first way many of us encountered this approach to storytelling is through F. Scott Fitzgerald's *The Great Gatsby*. Although Jay Gatsby is the main character of the novel, Nick Carraway—a peripheral character who shows up at critical times—tells the story. Nick is an observer rather than a direct participant in the action. This narrative technique allows the story to be told in a dispassionate voice, since the outsider (Nick) sometimes sees more and even knows more than the people directly involved in the story. Nick's point of view also serves as a stand-in for the reader, allowing her a more accurate and objective survey of each of the main characters' faults and failings.

### A survivor's tale

Conceiving of the narrator as the character who has lived to tell the tale is a powerful way to tell a story. This literary conceit has a long and venerable history, beginning with the Bible's Old Testament.

In the Book of Job, each of the four messengers that arrives to bring increasingly horrific news to the tragic hero ends his account with, "and I only am escaped alone to tell thee." That is a haunting refrain for any story.

Herman Melville opens *Moby-Dick* with the famous line, "Call me Ishmael." Here, the narrator is the lone survivor of Captain Ahab's mad quest to destroy the great white whale. And it is Ishmael who tells the story of what happened to the ill-fated crew of the *Pequod*.

So, before you lock yourself in to having the protagonist tell your first-person story, think about how your story might unfold if it were told from the point of view of another character—even a minor one. A singular advantage of using an observer-narrator is that the reader learns about the action at the same time the narrator does. Nothing is revealed before its time, an approach that might allow you to tell the story in a more interesting and compelling way.

## First-Person Moods

One of the pleasures of writing in first person is that you can create such a variety of moods. Serious and funny. Casual and formal. Ominous and inviting. Angry and gentle. It's all there for you to explore.

In *A Girl's Best Friend*, Elizabeth Young begins her chick lit novel with these lines:

> Though I say it myself, I made a lovely tart.
>
> From my wardrobe mirror she pouted back at me: Emerald Caprice, slapper with a heart of nine-karat gold plate and very good at games. Naughty school-girls with cabinet ministers, Miss Moneypenny to a bishop's Bond: you name it, Emerald had done it and taken notes. Just now she was about to publish her memoirs, go on talk shows, and sell excerpt rights to the Sunday papers.

In this brief opening, Young presents us with a sassy voice that is not only provocative, it's spiced with a dash of risqué. There's nothing heavy here. Just light fun.

At the flip side of the spectrum, Raymond Chandler creates a plain, straightforward, no-nonsense mood in his classic works of detective fiction. He's just giving you the facts, ma'am, telling it like it is when he begins *The Big Sleep*:

> It was about eleven o'clock in the morning, mid October, with the sun not shining and a look of hard wet rain in the clearness of the foothills. I was wearing my power-blue suit, with dark blue shirt, tie and display handkerchief, black brogues, black wool socks with dark blue clocks on them. I was neat, clean, shaved and sober, and I didn't care who knew it. I was everything the well-dressed private detective ought to be. I was calling on four million dollars.

Barbara Kingsolver creates a totally different mood in the opening of *The Poisonwood Bible*. There's more intensity here, a sense of danger that pulls the reader into the dark, tangled story. The ominous tone reflects tension, disturbance:

> Imagine a ruin so strange it must never have happened.
>
> First, picture the forest. I want you to be its conscience, the eyes in the trees. The trees are columns of slick, brindled bark like muscular animals overgrown beyond all reason. Every space is filled with life: delicate, poisonous frogs war-painted like skeletons, clutched in copulation, secreting the precious eggs onto dripping leaves. Vines strangling their own kin in the everlasting wrestle for sunlight. The breathing of monkeys. A glide of snake belly on branch. ... This forest eats itself and lives forever.

Three first-person books, three wildly contrasting moods and voices. The possibilities are endless. The decision you, the writer, must make is how to balance the advantages and disadvantages of first person in order to tell the best possible story.

## READING LIST
### Examples of First-Person Books

***Dead Until Dark*** by Charlaine Harris: If vampires with southern accents are your thing, read this mystery about Sookie—a southern cocktail waitress with an ability to read minds—who falls in love with a dashing vampire who doesn't allow her to read his.

***Lolita*** by Vladimir Nabokov: Humbert Humbert marries a woman in order to seduce her twelve-year-old daughter, Dolores, a.k.a. Lolita. Five years later, he kills the man who abducts Lolita. He then writes the story of his obsession as he awaits trial for murder.

***Bridget Jones's Diary*** by Helen Fielding: Bridget Jones, a thirtysomething editor in London, longs to meet Mr. Right. She's a woman who's smart and doesn't know it, and attractive but doesn't feel it. The novel is comprised of her diary, narrated in a voice both amusing and touching.

***Mount Misery*** by Samuel Shem: The narrator is a young psychiatrist who enters a three-year training program at a mental hospital outside Boston that caters to well-heeled wackos. Combining sharp comedy with probing tragedy, the author writes in a first-person voice filled with humor and wit along with insight and sensitivity.

## THIRD-PERSON, SINGLE POINT OF VIEW

In a way, third-person single—also called third-person limited—is the flip side of a first-person narration. The narrator stays with a single, designated character, telling the story exclusively from his single, designated viewpoint. You still can't get in anyone else's head or witness any action outside the knowledge of one particular character. The difference, however, is that the *I* becomes a *he* or a *she*.

If these approaches are so similar, you might be tempted to ask why you should bother leaving the first-person narrative at all. It's so cozy there. So familiar. You've already got a handle on that approach. Consider these reasons.

## Advantages of Third-Person, Single Point of View

- **The reader identifies with a specific character.** As in first person, this technique enlists the allegiance of the reader and invites a strong emotional identification with one specific character.

- **Your narrative horizons are expanded.** This shift in perspective is not as limiting as you might imagine—nor as restrictive as some people would have you believe. Here, you can devise one voice for the protagonist and a different one for the narrator, giving you the latitude to play voice and tone against each other. For instance, if the narrator of the story is a spurned woman, but the tone of the book—the story being told—is magical and elegiac, the interplay between these different moods can create an intriguing story. Here, as in first person, you can create a narrative shift to another location by having the character imagine a distant scenario.

- **Your ability to offer emotional insights is deepened.** Some people believe telling your story from this point of view diminishes your ability to evoke the feelings, thoughts, and passions of the hero. Not so. It's just as easy to get into the head of a character in third-person narration as it is in first person. To accomplish this you must remain conscious of showing (not telling) how the character feels. But you can also shift out of the head of the single character and offer a wider perspective on the action, adding layers to the narrative and offering a deeper understanding of the emotions expressed.

- **Your opportunity to interpret events is enlarged.** The narrator, as well as the viewpoint character, can comment on events, allowing the author greater latitude in exploring and explaining events.

## Disadvantages of Third-Person, Single Point of View

- **Your viewpoint is limited to one character.** Just as in first person, you can still only tell your story through one character's eyes.

- **It's harder to balance the narration.** It's a greater challenge to balance the author's voice with the third-person, singular voice that is viewing the events.

Stacked against the advantages of this POV, however, I don't view these drawbacks as inhibiting.

Third-person, single is an intriguing way to tell a story—especially if you want a pinpoint focus on the events in the life of one character. James Joyce did this to great effect in "The Dead." Depending on the voice of the author and the mood of the protagonist, you can create the same variety of feelings that you can in first person, evoking either complementary or contradictory moods as you do it.

### READING LIST
Examples of Third-Person, Single Point of View

**The Harry Potter series** by J.K. Rowling: All the Harry Potter books are written with a third-person, single point of view, and yet they manage to open the vision of the narrator to a wider fictional world by showing (not telling) what others think and feel.

*The Portrait of a Lady* by Henry James: is the story of Isabel Archer, a woman determined not to sacrifice her independence for the sake of marriage. But she does. And the ramifications of her choice color the rest of her life.

*Saturday* by Ian McEwan: This is a Saturday in the life of Henry Perowne, a British neurosurgeon, set against a backdrop of anti-war demonstrations and a dangerous confrontation. After making it through a chaotic twenty-four hours, the doctor ends his day with love.

# THIRD-PERSON, MULTIPLE POINT OF VIEW

In third-person multiple, the author tells the story in the third person (i.e., he said, she said), but from more than one point of view. If you want to focus on two or three characters, this is the narrative approach to choose.

Again, don't be misled into thinking you must sacrifice the intimacy of feelings and the connection with the reader when you use this voice. It does, however, require more effort to explore hidden places and maintain the bond between each point-of-view character and the reader. But you can achieve this by entering the character's thoughts and showing his actions and reactions to a variety of circumstances.

## Advantages of Third-Person, Multiple Point of View

- **You can convey a fuller story.** Instead of telling the story from just one point of view, this method allows you to expand your horizons and witness other events without losing the tight focus on two or three main characters.

- **You can get into the head of more than one character.** Instead of being limited to the thoughts and feelings of one single character, you can deepen the insight into the emotional state of several characters—thereby deepening the reader's appreciation of the events and dilemmas you present.

- **You have a better chance for reader identification.** If you have several characters who play central roles in the plot, the reader can experience the thoughts and feelings of all these characters. This increases the understanding of the conflicts and allows the writer to state the case for more than one person's point of view.

- **You can create a conflict in the reader's mind.** If you paint full portraits of two or three characters, you can then set up questions for the reader to consider: *Who is right in this situation? Which path would I choose? How would I behave here? Even though I identify with this character, I can understand that one.* Feelings such as these keep the reader interested in the story, since he wants to know how the conflict will be resolved and which character will be proven right.

- **It's easier to paint the world in shades of gray.** In case you hadn't noticed, the last time our world was painted in black and white was sometime around World War II. Or at least during that era, we managed to ignore the gray. Today, in spite of concerted efforts to the contrary—and because of the explosion of communication possibilities— we all now walk in a world painted in shades of gray. For instance, in June 2008, the U.S. Supreme Court ruled in a 5–4 decision that the death penalty could not be applied in the case of child rape. If you were to create a novel based on the actions reflected in the opposing opinions in this case, both points of view could be expressed in a third-person, multiple POV story. Characters might ask themselves *is any capital punishment moral?* Is the rape of an eight-year-old girl less heinous than the swift homicide of a sixty-eight-year-old man? The advantage here is that you've got the freedom to wander among minds—those who agree and disagree and those who are torn between the two. This makes third-person, multiple POV a perfect voice to use when you want to delve into the layers of an uncertain world.

## Disadvantages of Third-Person, Multiple Point of View

• **You can lose your pinpoint focus on one character.** Once you spread the point of view to other characters, you run the risk of diluting the reader's identification with the character. However, I don't consider this much of a disadvantage, since careful writing can prevent this from happening.

• **You must pay special attention to delineating your voices.** If you switch between several points of view, it's critical to be clear about who is speaking in each scene and who is witnessing each event. The reader should never have to pause and figure out whose point of view is being expressed.

### READING LIST
Examples of Third-Person, Multiple Books

*The Maytrees* by Annie Dillard: The author tells the story of a family from the points of view of three people: Lou, the wife; Toby, the husband who takes a sojourn of twenty years with Deary; and Pete, their son. The novel is about love in all of its combinations and permutations; how it transforms and is transforming over the span of a lifetime.

*A Thousand Splendid Suns* by Khaled Hosseini: This story is told from the point of view of two Afghani women who are condemned to a life of marriage to the same barbaric man whose idea of a commonplace activity is beating his wives.

*Plainsong* by Kent Haruf: A lovely choral work of a novel, it weaves the stories of eight different characters into a quiet, amusing, and touching drama that takes place in the high plains of Colorado.

The Alexandria Quartet by Lawrence Durrell: Instead of one book, let me recommend Durrell's four brilliant novels, *Justine*, *Balthazar*, *Mountolive*, and *Clea*. They explore the same sequence of events that occur before and during World War II. Each book is narrated from a different character's point of view. Part quantum universe and part Freud, the Alexandria Quartet can and should be read as one novel.

## Ways to Distinguish Multiple Points of View

Whether you're considering multiple first-person narrators or third-person multiple POV, here are some tips to help you construct a clearer narrative.

**Separate the points of view.** When you shift from one viewpoint character to the other, create a break with a double space or other marker to indicate change.

**Change the POV at scene changes.** Narrate separate scenes from separate points of view.

**Set up parallel responses.** Write a story in which the hero behaves one way in "real" life and then secretly responds in a totally different way in her journal or diary.

**Try the epistolary approach.** Tell first-person stories through the exchange of letters, postcards, or e-mail between multiple characters.

**Set up a pattern of change.** Alternate chapters or scenes so the reader comes to expect the shift from one character to the other. This technique not only offers clarity, it creates a sense of anticipation in the reader about what the other character will think or say or do next.

Note: Try to vary the pattern occasionally so the reader doesn't become bored with the predictability.

**Create timelines.** If you have three or four characters telling the story, break the book up into clearly delineated chronological timelines in which you tell the story of one specific character.

For instance, you could do this with days or months. *September: Lisa and Rhonda. November: Pat and Vibul. May: Lisa, Pat, Rhonda, Vibul.* Each person has a chapter or a section in September and November and May. In the last section, all their stories come together.

**Label locations.** For instance, you would head your chapters *YWCA: Tilly, Heather, Sheila; Fashion Arena Shopping Center: Sheila, Tilly; MacArthur Park: Sheila, Heather.* When you do this, a new voice takes over the story when the location changes. You shift to a new locale, and you shift to a new Point of View.

**Alternate chapters.** If your events are happening simultaneously and two or more characters are telling about them, alternate chapters between the different points of view. Clarify the fact that the actions are happening alongside each other by noting the time, day, or date or some other significant event. The last chapter should bring the storylines together.

**Split the pages.** Place Jack's commentary on the left-hand page and Annie's on the right. Or ... one technique, artfully crafted by Carol Shields in *Happenstance*, is to have one story read from front to back; then turn the book over and read back to front.

**Alternate chapters and voices.** If you're telling the story in a sequential fashion, have Mohammed narrate the first chapter, Gabriella the second, and Jenny the third.

**Alternate emphasis.** Give the voice of your main character greater emphasis, with the secondary characters commenting at the beginning or end of each chapter.

## Tips for the Skillful Use of Multiple Points of View

**Choose dominating characters.** When you tell the story from multiple points of view, you can maintain reader allegiance by having one or two characters dominate the action.

**Emphasize main characters.** When using multiple characters, don't spread your story so evenly that you deprive the reader of identifying with one or two main characters.

**Beware of detachment.** Beware of a voice that is so removed from the action that you dilute the reader's ability to identify with the characters.

**Shift deliberately.** Make the shifts from character to character early on in the story so the reader comes to expect these changes.

**Stick with one point of view within the scene.** With rare exceptions, do not change your point of view in the middle of a scene. It's too disconcerting for the reader.

**Parcel out information.** Beware of divulging information that will temper the suspense in the story.

**Keep characters in check.** Just because you can have your characters go anywhere and do anything, that doesn't mean you should. If they stray from the essentials of the narrative, you dilute the focus and lose your reader.

**No gratuitous shifts to other points of view.** If the viewpoint of the other character doesn't make a significant contribution to the scene or the story, don't use it.

**Avoid the trap of a mandatory revelation.** Shifting the point of view to other characters can force you to reveal information you don't want disclosed—information that would spoil the surprise. For instance, if the character knows a secret about something he has witnessed, you can't withhold this information if you shift into his thoughts and feelings.

# OMNISCIENT POINT OF VIEW

If playing God is your thing, have I got a point of view for you!

In contrast to the third-person, multiple POV that allows the writer to get into the heads of several characters, the omniscient narrator's voice speaks with a power all its own. Here, the narrator uses the fairy tale voice—think "Once upon a time ..."

Omniscient means that the narrator is all-seeing, all-knowing. Like Santa, he knows when you—and everybody else—have been naughty and he knows when you've been nice. Furthermore, the narrator is allowed to offer his own opinion about unfolding events. Stories told from an omniscient point of view offer multiple ways of looking at a given incident. If five people witness one incident, the writer can explore and express not only how each character feels at that moment, but what each person sees and remembers. And at any moment in the narration, the omniscient voice can offer its own opinion about the unfolding events.

These days, the omniscient point of view isn't used as frequently as the other storytelling techniques. In spite of the fact that it allows the author the greatest range, it is fraught with pitfalls. Unless this approach is executed with consummate skill, the omniscient viewpoint can weaken a story and dilute the reader's allegiance to any single character. Furthermore, if you're writing for younger readers, the omniscient voice can be downright confusing.

That said, if your goal is to get into the heads of multiple characters and use the narrator as a separate voice, this is the approach to choose. Here, your story isn't limited to the world as witnessed through the eyes of one or two characters. The viewpoint is godlike, and the narrator's voice is often stronger than the individual characters. Leo Tolstoy's *Anna Karenina* is a perfect example of a sweeping story told from a powerful omniscient point of view that still embraces characters who present strong, competing voices of their own.

## Advantages of the Omniscient Point of View

- **You can get into lots of characters' heads.** You can present your story or scene from many viewpoints and convey the private thoughts and feelings of multiple characters.

- **You can tell your story from a broader perspective.** Since you're not limited to what one or two characters experience, you have a wider scope in how to present your story.

- **You can play one character's feelings off against another.** If three people witness the same scene, you can show why each feels the way he or she does and how their ideas conflict with one another.

## Disadvantages of the Omniscient Point of View

- **You risk diluting the reader's identification with any singular character.** When too many stories are told from too many points of view, a reader can lose interest in any one character.

- **It's too easy for the reader to become confused about who feels what.** Too many individual stories open up the reader to a mixture of views and opinions. Unless the characters are wildly distinctive, their feelings, thoughts, and motives can become blurred.

- **You can lose the inherent passion of a story that is limited to one or two points of view.** If everyone has strong feelings about a given incident, all the feelings can be diluted.

- **It's easy for the reader to lose focus on the heart of the story.** If there are too many stories to tell, one story has a hard time dominating the action and capturing the reader.

## READING LIST
### Examples of Omniscient Books

*Bel Canto* by Ann Patchett: The story moves in and out of the psyches of terrorists and captives alike as a hostage drama is played out against a backdrop of opera and budding love stories.

*The Bluest Eye* by Toni Morrison: This is the story of one little girl in a family burdened with a cloak of ugliness.

*The Hitchhiker's Guide to the Galaxy* by Douglas Adams: The book roams through the hearts and minds of multiple characters as civilizations clash and mingle.

*Cannery Row* by John Steinbeck: Steinbeck uses the third-person, omniscient point of view as he tells the tales of what happens to the characters who work in the canneries in Monterey, California.

*The Quartzsite Trip* by William Hogan: Here the author uses the omniscient point of view with extraordinary skill to tell the tale of thirty-six high school seniors who take a class trip to Quartzsite, Arizona, with a teacher who revels in the pleasures and perils of playing God.

## ADDENDUM: SECOND-PERSON, SINGULAR POINT OF VIEW

Every once in a while a book is written in the second-person, singular point of view—i.e., *you* do this and *you* see that. This narrative approach is used for a specific reason, such as creating a story in which the reader becomes the main character. My partner and I did this when we wrote our series of Which Way Books for kids. The voice is intriguing to use, and I hope to do it again if I'm given the chance.

In *Bright Lights, Big City*, Jay McInerney opens his book with:

> You are not the kind of guy who would be at a place like this at this time of the morning. But here you are, and you cannot say that the terrain is entirely unfamiliar, although the details are fuzzy. You are at a nightclub talking to a girl with a shaved head. The club is either Heartbreak or the Lizard Lounge. All might come clear if you could just slip into the bathroom and do a little more Bolivian Marching Powder.

Here, the author creates a powerful sense of immediacy in his ability to pull the reader into the novel and become a participant in the self-absorbed, cocaine-fueled life of a lost young man.

## READING LIST
### Examples of Second-Person Books

**"The Haunted Mind"** by Nathaniel Hawthorne: In one of his *Twice-Told Tales*, Hawthorne addresses the reader as he describes what it feels like to shift into that "intermediate space" between sleeping and waking. It is here, the narrator says, that the spirits haunt you before they "dissipate the fragments of your slumber."

*Ulysses* by James Joyce: Joyce intermittently uses a second-person-singular voice as protagonist Leopold Bloom moves through eighteen chapters set in Dublin, each with its own theme based on characters from Homer's *Odyssey*—and ending with Molly Bloom's sensual, sensational, and shocking soliloquy. Tackling this book isn't for sissies. It's crammed with word play, parodies, puzzles, literary allusions, and stream of consciousness passages designed to drive scholars berserk.

But if you're looking for an intellectual and literary challenge, this is the book for you.

*Half Asleep in Frog Pajamas* by Tom Robbins: The second-person voice seems to attract iconoclasts, and Robbins is no exception. The author mixes the psychedelic with the mysterious and steeps them in word play as he takes a Seattle commodities broker and plants him in the middle of a mad, far-out weekend.

# MEAT AND POTATOES

So there you have it: Everything you need to know about the various points of view. If you find it all too confusing, just remember that point of view encompasses two critical questions:

Meat: *Who* tells the story.

Potatoes: *How* that story is told.

As you've seen, the choices you make will have a radical effect on the story you tell. Don't be afraid to experiment with different approaches. The goal isn't to be right the first time you try. The goal is to be effective and memorable the last time you try.

## Questions to Ask Yourself About Your Story

- Which character or characters would tell the story in the most interesting way?

- How would my story change if it were told from a single point of view? From multiple points of view?

- Can I expand or limit point of view to increase suspense?

- What information must I include or delete in order to shift points of view?

- What are the advantages and disadvantages of the different narrative voices?

- What mood am I trying to convey? Formal? Informal? Casual? Ominous? Playful?

- Do I want the narrator's voice to act as another character or to fade into the background?

## 15

# INNER AND OUTER DIALOGUE
## Authenticity and Credibility

---

*Dialogue is a very useful tool to reveal things about people, and novels are about people and what they do to each other.*

—Thomas McGuane

I have a friend whose father is a noted screenwriter. My friend tells me that when he was growing up, he and his brother would be sitting in the back seat of the car as their father drove them to the beach, and suddenly their dad would utter some total non sequitur. Then, while carrying on an ostensible conversation with his sons, this man would enter into an extended, mumbled discourse with unseen people, working out dialogue between characters for one movie scene after another.

I have a hunch that lots of writers (including me) "hear" thoughts and dialogue as they move through their days. You don't have to be working on a specific scene or project to do this. You just have to listen to the thoughts that cross your mind in a constant stream throughout your conscious hours. If you don't hear them as a matter of course, make an effort to access them. Do yoga, deep breathing, meditation, or other exercises that still your mind. It's in the midst of silence that the voices speak loudest.

In the interest of full disclosure, I should tell you that my visual imagination is limited to nonexistent. It's a brain burp of some sort and I'm stuck with it. As a consequence, most of my thoughts come in words, not pictures. I ramble through my days with a running monologue playing in my head. I not only hear dialogue, I speak it out loud. Lest you suspect I'm the crazy lady given to walking along the beach and chatting with imaginary friends, I hasten to assure you that I used to talk to myself, but I don't anymore. Now I talk to my dog.

## TRICKS OF THE TRADE
### In Praise of White Space

There are lots of studies concerning the layout of a page and its readability factor. On a practical level, dialogue offers a special advantage to the reader because it opens up a page. In my opinion, this visual advantage is critical. There's a value in white space. A page of one or two paragraphs filled with solid print intimidates a reader. For some, this sight can discourage reading the book altogether.

I suspect lots of book browsers (I'm one of them) recoil at the sight of a solid page of prose. There are hundreds of thousands of books out there that people can choose to read. The solid print problem is why—when I'm not using dialogue—I try to write in short paragraphs. The visual relief that paragraph indents create makes the page more inviting and the reading experience more accessible and enjoyable.

# THOUGHTS ON THOUGHT

Dialogue comes in two distinct flavors: inner and outer. Just as speech reveals character, so does thought.

When a character responds to a given situation, his thoughts should reflect who he truly is. This doesn't mean that a shy kid thinks only shy thoughts. In fact, his thoughts could reflect the opposite of what he's saying or doing. He can say whatever he wants to suit his audience but what's not going to change is his core—what he's thinking, regardless of what he's saying.

Let's say David, a shy introvert, has been cornered on the street by a gangbanger. Even though he's acquiescing to the bully, David could be thinking He-Man thoughts, such as *I'll tear you limb from limb. Someday, I'm gonna beat the crap out of you.*

On the other hand, Alison might talk tough, but her thoughts would reflect her fear. When confronted by the same bully, she might say, "Get away from me, you creep!" all while thinking, *Oh God, don't let me start crying now. Please don't let me cry.*

Whether the protagonist's thoughts work in tandem with his actions or run counter to them, whether he has a rich fantasy life or one rooted in reality, make certain his character is revealed by what and how he thinks—not just by how he behaves. Although not every writer does it, using thoughts can be a powerful tool for furthering the story and explaining its subtext. I would caution you, however, to use this tool sparingly. Sometimes you can stay inside your character's head too much, telling instead of showing. You can end up avoiding the creation of a physical scene (and therefore *action*, which is critical to plot) and depriving the reader of discovering some of the subtleties of the story for himself.

## The Mechanics of Thought

It used to be that when a character was thinking, the way you defined this inner process was by writing, Jamie thought this ... or Liz thought that .... These days, some writers have turned their backs on that tradition and are putting thoughts in italics.

This removes the necessity for the tag line and allows for more creative room to move.

Italics for thought are perfectly acceptable. Quotation marks are *not*. I once edited a book in which the author insisted on putting thoughts in quotation marks. There were multiple instances in which I couldn't distinguish between spoken and imagined dialogue. It's important to make sure your reader understands the difference, especially because thoughts can be interjected alongside dialogue without stopping to define them as thought.

Another approach that contemporary writers use is simply beginning the thought with a capital letter, as in: As soon as I kissed my ex-boyfriend I could hear my head screaming, What are you thinking?!?

The seamless transition between exposition and thought can be found in countless books. But just for the record, here are a couple of different approaches to guide you:

"An Irrevocable Diameter" by Grace Paley:

> Once we were allowed to speak to each other, she said, "What a wild Indian you turned into, Charles."
> Was she kidding? Was she proud? Why did she even care?

*After* by Robert Anderson:

> Toward evening, when they told me Fran was on her way down from the recovery room, I said to myself, "I will block out my reactions. I will simply be there when she first opens her eyes, when she asks the questions."

*So Long, Princess* by Barbara Brooker:

> "When you're ready, men will find you. And when you begin working, get out in the real world, you will meet men."
> *Sure, sure, easy for her to say. Look at her, all thirty-five and beautiful, a professional person. What does she know about menopause?*

# THOUGHTS ON DIALOGUE

Contrary to what lots of writers assume, dialogue shouldn't be a replica of speech. Reading a book that reflects how people actually speak could be a serious drag.

"Like, you know, uhh, like aaa maybe that wouldn't be such a umm sterling idea."

The goal of writing dialogue is not to mimic how people speak; the goal of writing dialogue is to create the *illusion* of authenticity. Try sitting in a restaurant or park for a few hours and listening to the dialogue around you. Then try reproducing snippets of a stranger's tone or rhythm or vocabulary. This might be a good place to start if you're having a hard time with dialogue. Just omit the *wells*, *uhms*, and *uhhs*.

## Dialogue as Character

Each of your main characters should have a different way of using words. Just as you and I speak differently, so should your characters.

Consider the following voices:

Abby: "I don't give a rat's ass about that."

Steve: "Why don't you remind me why I should care?"

Ryan: "Why should I think this is important?"

Joe: "I'm outa here."

Isabel: "Caring's not a concept that intrigues me enough to embrace it."

Kevin: "Why on **earth** should someone in my position bother with that?"

Melissa: "Like, I should waste my time with this?"

Mark: "Forget it."

Cybele: "That's not worth thinking about."

All of these characters are saying the same thing in a different way. Some people ask questions, others make statements. Each character you create should have his or her distinctive voice. This is what makes dialogue true and what makes fiction compelling.

Before you start writing a scene that contains dialogue, it might be helpful to free-write a half a page or so in each character's voice so you have the distinct personalities in the forefront of your mind. How would she "translate" common phrases like "I don't care," "Listen to what I'm telling you," or "That hurts my feelings"?

# SIX STRATEGIES FOR DIALOGUE

You can't really divorce dialogue from character. Like salt and pepper, they belong together. Once your characters come alive in your imagination, their dialogue will flow onto the page with a greater ease.

## 1. Create Dialogue That Reveals Character and Mood

There's a difference between "I dunno," and "I haven't the foggiest notion." Not only can speech reflect who your character is, it can also reveal secrets. The slight stutter, the hesitation, can change the entire tone of a scene.

## 2. Invent an Authentic Voice for Each Character

In theory, you shouldn't have to identify who's speaking because each character's voice should be distinct. That's not always possible. But it is possible to make certain you believe what each character is saying and how he says it. As you write your dialogue, ask yourself if the words are being true to who the character is. Would a forty-year-old woman from a farm in Nebraska ask, "Wazzup, bro? How's it hanging?" I don't think so.

Then there's the guy who's just a little too enthusiastic about seeing the movie his blind date has chosen: "Cool! I've always wanted to see a chick flick!"

## 3. Avoid Trendy Slang

The only exceptions to this are if it's in keeping with your character or the time period of your story. Slang can date your book. Today's cool words can be tomorrow's passé lingo. *Neat* and *keen* became *rad*, which became *cool*, which became *sweet,* which became .... You get the point.

If you have a fantasy about your book staying in print for a long time, don't tie your narrative to dated words or trendy language unless you're trying to lock your story and characters into a specific time and place. For example, many of the popular young adult series like *Gossip Girl* depend on language and behavior that's *en vogue*. The decision to use slang should be based on your market and audience.

## 4. Establish Distinct Voices

Make certain your voices are distinct. John doesn't speak like Dolly who doesn't speak like Clio. Even with kids who try to speak alike, their voices have a different rhythm and different emphasis. "There's no way I'm going to do that," is distinct from, "No way am I doing that."

## 5. Give the Speaker Something to Do

Define action and character by having the speaker do something. Rather than putting all the description in the exposition, tag some of it onto dialogue so you can keep the action of the scene moving. It's pretty boring to read about two talking heads floating in empty space.

> "I'm not nervous," Dirk said as he glanced at the door.

> "What makes you think I'm going to die?" Ron asked, taking another puff of his cigarette.

This kind of "business" can be used to reveal character or give a hint about the action. Although this amplification of action is effective, use it judiciously. Too much of the same thing becomes tedious.

## 6. Speak Dialogue Out Loud

When I create dialogue, I repeat the words out loud as I write. The difference between how words sound in your head and how they sound coming out of your mouth is the difference between artifice and authenticity.

To tell the truth, I repeat most of my writing out loud. I also hear it in my imagination as I write. Whether it's dialogue or exposition, it helps my creative process to hear how the words hang together, how the sentences sound before they've received the final blessing of the printed page.

## FIVE NO-NOS OF DIALOGUE

When dialogue rings false, it sets off alarms in the head of the reader. It also signals to an editor that the writer is a rookie. So do whatever you can to avoid the following rookie mistakes.

### 1. Beware of Repetition
Say it once and say it well. It doesn't take long for dialogue to become tedious. As in, "There's not a chance I'm going to do that. Not enough money in the world to make me. Not gonna happen."

### 2. Avoid Fancy Tag Lines
Keep your tag lines simple. The eye is accustomed to skipping over the *said*s as in "he said," "she said," so the pace of the dialogue stays brisk. On the other hand, "he opined," "she questioned," "she queried," "he inquired," and "she replied" jump off the page and interfere with the narrative flow. They also alert an editor that the dialogue is written by a novice. This doesn't mean you can never use a fancy tag line. Just use them sparingly and for good reason.

### 3. Ditch Inaccurate Tag Line Verbs
"Guess again!" he laughed/grimaced/wept. None of these words describe the actual act of speaking; they describe what the character is doing when he speaks. Try it this way instead: "Guess again," he said with a laugh.

### 4. Don't Use Proper Names to Distinguish Speakers
Lots of writers new to the game think they can avoid tag lines by using proper names in the dialogue. As in:

> "Well, Donna, I think it's your dog that's causing the problem."
>
> "Why would you say that, Chris? Mine isn't the dog that peed on the doormat."

Unless they're trying to make a specific point, people rarely use proper names in dialogue. This is not a clever way to avoid using *said*. This makes the prose sound stiff. And it's another way for an editor to identify you as a rookie.

## 5. Resist Preaching Through Dialogue

In their urge to moralize, sometimes writers think they can sneak a message into the dialogue and nobody will know the difference. Wrong.

> "I don't know why he smokes so much dope. Doesn't he know that it's addictive?"
>
> "I just read a study that says smoking pot changes your chromosomes—not to mention the fact that heavy use impairs your memory."

What's the reader's response to this preachy dialogue? Rolled eyes, disdain, and the permanently closed covers of a book. If you want to convey this message in your story, the best advice is to write a story whose characters and actions demonstrate the anti–drug message.

## DIALOGUE DOUBLE-CHECKLIST

As you write your story, read all the dialogue out loud, making certain there's a natural feel and rhythm to the words. If you stumble over a phrase, rewrite it. Once you've finished the scene, check your work with these questions:

- Does this dialogue feel authentic?

- Does the dialogue belong to this specific character?

- Have I struck the right mood?

- Have I conveyed what I want to say in the best way possible?

- Is there anything I can do to tighten the dialogue?

- Do I believe what the characters are saying?

# PART IV

# INTERIOR DESIGNS

## 16

# KEEPING YOUR PROMISE

## Premise, Theme, and Moral

---

*No one can write decently who is distrustful
of the reader's intelligence, or whose attitude
is patronizing.*

—E.B. White

When I discussed endings in chapter ten, I talked about the importance of fulfilling the promise and expectations set up by your inciting incident. When you write the opening scene of your story, never forget that you are offering a contract to your reader—a promise you must not break.

And when you create a contract, you can't *sort of* keep your promise. There's no wiggle room here. You can't start out with a thriller introduction and move into a cozy sibling drama. The reader depends on you to stick to your writing guns.

Also inherent in this promise is your willingness to remove yourself from the story in order to let a character's action speak for itself. The interjection of the author's voice and opinions on those of the character intrudes on the narrative dream and dilutes the credibility of the story.

The promise in that first scene colors every authorial decision you make concerning the background of your story, as well as its scope and structure. Because the promise is so integral to the overall plot, it's important to examine and understand all the aspects that make up this agreement before you write. That said, you make your promise in four basic ways:

1. With your premise.
2. With your theme.
3. With your voice.
4. With your tone.

We'll examine premise and theme in this chapter and save voice and tone for the next.

## THE BASIC PREMISE

Lots of people confuse theme and premise. It's easy to do since the two are kissing cousins and will blur if you so much as blow on them. With that in mind, it's a good idea to distinguish these two discrete concepts so you can construct your plot and keep the thematic arc of your story on track.

The word *premise* is derived from Medieval Latin. *Missa* or *misse* means "put"; *pre* means "before": "To put before."

In our context, premise, as James N. Frey defines it in *How to Write a Damn Good Novel*, is "a statement of what happens to the characters as a result of the core conflict in the story ... Does every dramatic story have a premise? Yes. One and only one premise? Yes. You can't ride two bicycles at the same time and you can't prove two premises at the same time."

Working with this definition, the premise of "The Three Little Pigs" is not: Three innocents threatened by a scary monster. Nor is it: The merits of various construction techniques in middle-income housing. The premise, Frey says, is: "Foolishness leads to death, and wisdom leads to happiness."

Another example of premise can be found in one of Aesop's fables, "The Fox and the Crow." In the story, a Crow manages to snag a piece of cheese and settle on the branch of a tree to eat it. But when the Fox sees the cheese, he wants that tasty morsel for himself. Living up to his wily reputation, the Fox convinces the Crow he wants to hear her sing. Succumbing to flattery, the Crow opens her mouth and begins to caw. And the cheese falls into the hands of the Fox.

The premise? If you can't get what you want by asking, you can get it by flattering. The fable demonstrates this premise in its actions.

So, in short, the premise is what your book is about. Premise is *not* the plot. It is the *underlying idea* that is demonstrated by the plot. Ideally, you should establish the premise of your story before you even begin writing. If you can do this, you will save yourself untold creative angst.

Think of premise as the foundation of your plot, the essential truth you want to convey. And the truth that gives shape to your story and meaning to the lives of your characters. Premise has a beginning—an idea—but it also has an ending—a conclusion. Before you begin to write your book, try to determine what your premise is and then build your story upon it.

To get you started thinking about your own premise, here are some time-tested examples, demonstrated again and again in a variety of unique plots:

Premise: A life of petty crime leads to a life in prison.

Premise: Transforming a life takes a lifetime of work.

Premise: Where there's a will, there's a way.

Premise: The first love you have is the last love you remember.

Premise: When you betray a friend, you lose a friend.

Premise: When you lose a friend, you lose your history.

Now try defining the premise of your story in one sentence. Want one last example? The premise of *The Great Gatsby* is, very simply: When you pray for something, beware of answered prayers.

You might not believe it's worth your time to ponder the meaning and ramifications of premise. But if you think of premise as the most fundamental idea in your book that must be proven by the actions of your characters, it becomes clear that the premise is the connective tissue that binds your story together. It also keeps your plot on track and prevents it from falling apart.

James N. Frey says, "[E]very good premise should contain an element of *character* which through *conflict* leads to a *conclusion* ... A dramatic story is the transformation of character through crisis; the premise is a succinct statement of that transformation."

If your protagonist "tells" you he must take a certain action, ask yourself if his behavior proves the premise. If your hero does something totally out of character, ask yourself if you can find a way to make this behavior reflect your premise.

## VARIATIONS ON A THEME

The theme of your book is the narrative concept behind your story—the idea explored within the context of what your book is about. Theme is *not* the premise. Nor is it the message or the moral. The key difference between premise and theme is that there is only one premise in a story, but there can be multiple themes.

Think of premise as the warp and woof of a tapestry—those sturdy strands without which you cannot weave your story. On the other hand, themes are the dominant threads woven through the warp and woof that, when they come together, create the desired picture.

One theme of a book might be the tug of war between love and hate. Another might be the exploration of what makes a man courageous or how you draw the line between loyalty and betrayal.

In *Ordinary Heroes*, for instance, Scott Turow tells the tale of an unlikely bond forged between a JAG lawyer in Patton's Third Army in World War II and a Resistance hero suspected of being a counterspy.

The *premise* of this book might be: When confronted with facts, the truth wears many guises.

The *themes* of the book are: the transcendent might of the will, the price we pay for courage, the hidden faces of war, the many facets of truth, and the heroic struggle to reconcile the reality of death with the demands of life.

These themes are represented in the behavior of the characters and the elements of the plot.

Theme is not a one-sided reflection of a character or situation. Theme has multiple dimensions and is developed in multiple ways—light and dark, inside and outside, upside down and right side up. One theme echoes an earlier theme. One theme evolves from another.

To borrow an illustration from another art form, let's examine the concept of theme as it applies to music. When a composer creates variations on a theme, or primary melody, he might compose three or four different versions of the same melody.

For instance, the theme of the fourth movement of Franz Schubert's Trout Quintet is the melody he wrote for a poem called "Die Forelle" by Christian Friedrich Daniel Schubart.

At the opening, the first violin sets the theme for the entire movement. Then the piano joins in with more ornamentation, accompanied by triplet rhythm. Soon the voice transfers to the viola, now accompanied by a stronger continuo from the bass and piano. Then full lower strings shift into a minor variation on the same theme that moves to the cello while the piano plays a more melodious andante, still in minor key. Finally, in the last statement, there's a lyrical return to the first violin and cello that ends with a quiet finish.

Each of these variations plays off one single central theme. Yet each is different, each is distinct.

A literary theme is developed in similar fashion—in repeated echoes and variations on the original. In one scene a writer might write about love and redemption in a positive light. Then he shifts to the dark side of love manifested in obsession, possession, and death.

Joy, vision, strength, weakness, creativity, disappointment, longing, rejection, fantasy, love, loss, fear, grief, death, hope.

All the aspects of our lives and our behavior that are an integral part of the human condition become transformed into themes in the hands of the writer.

## AND THE MORAL OF THE STORY IS ...

A moral is a lesson, a teaching. In storytelling, the moral often involves overtly judging the good or bad behavior of one or more of the characters—a lesson directed specifically at the reader. These are most obvious in classic fables and folktales and in mythology.

If you look at the "moral" of the story as a quality exemplified in the behavior and attitudes of a character, then of course you can include this in a story. However, a moral steeped in sermonizing is a major no-no.

My one-word advice to anyone who sets out to write a story with a stated lesson is: Don't. Aesop could get away with it. We can't. Readers of fiction these days are savvy and discerning. Most of them read to be introduced to other worldviews and sets of human experiences and to arrive at their own conclusions about those things—not to be preached to. Fiction used as a personal sounding board almost always reads flat and false. Worse than that, moralizing storytelling is all about the *author's* agenda, and as a writer, your primary responsibility is constructing an authentic experience for your *reader*. This obvious selfishness is why readers will deem your unread book an excellent source of kindling if they catch a whiff of authorial preaching.

Avoiding a moral doesn't preclude your ability to impart specific ideas in your book any more than it precludes your ability to convey the fact that there are consequences—from amusing to tragic—to the decisions we make. But you must communicate these ideas through actions and reactions of characters, and not through the author preaching to the reader ... or through one character preaching to another. In short, if you ditch the preaching you can keep the message.

# KEEPING YOUR WORD

Promise, premise, and theme: In and of themselves, these issues seem insignificant compared to the challenge of structuring and writing an entire book. But it is these very issues—the subtleties that indicate a writer is in full command of his work—that lift the story above the crowd and make it a book to respect and remember.

Consider your story. Then write down the answers to the following questions:

1. What is the promise I want to make to the reader?

 • How do I make that promise?

 • How do I keep that promise?

2. What is the premise of my book?

 • Define this in one sentence.

 • How do the characters reflect my premise?

3. What are the themes of my book?

 • In what characters and actions are these themes expressed?

Before you sit down to revise, use this checklist to:

 • Make certain your premise is set firmly in your mind.

 • Evaluate the promise you make to your reader.

 • Analyze how the actions and feelings of your characters reflect your premise.

 • Define the themes of your story and how they are manifested in the actions of your characters and the elements of the plot.

 • Remove all traces of any moral or lesson you feel compelled to teach.

## 17

# THE PROMISE CONTINUED

## Voice and Tone

---

*A strong narrative voice creates a feeling in the
reader that the writer knows what he or she is
talking about. It creates trust.*

—James N. Frey

To the casual observer, voice and tone are one and the same.
Like those pesky kissing cousins premise and theme (discussed
in the previous chapter), voice and tone are interconnected
and often function more as twins than as cousins. Occasionally, they even behave like siblings—agreeing with each other
one minute and fighting each other the next. Both, however,
contribute to the art of storytelling and shape the promise you
make to your reader. Boiled down to their essence, voice and
tone can be defined in the following way:

*Voice* is the *quality* of the narration, regardless of whether it's
told in first or third person. Is the voice you choose to tell the
story casual and friendly, or is it dark and scary?

*Tone* is the atmosphere of the book. Tone can be threatening, as in a thriller, or light and airy, as in a chick lit book.

Working with these definitions, we can examine each narrative feature separately.

## VOICE LESSONS

Now that you have a handle on the structural design of your book, it's time to decide how you're going to tell your story. This is your chance to become someone else: to put on a mask and become a clown, to experience what it's like to live in the skin of the opposite sex, or to inhabit the dark heart of a stranger.

The voice you choose to write with will either belong to a removed narrator or to a character in the book. You've got lots of options. Do you want to be ironic or comic? Serious, detached, or entertaining? Take a look at these openings and how they establish the voice.

Raymond Chandler cornered the market on tough-guy detectives in 1938. To wit: the opening of his short story, "Red Wind":

> There was a desert wind blowing that night. It was one of those hot dry Santa Anas that come down through the mountain passes and curl your hair and make your nerves jump and your skin itch. On nights like that every booze party ends in a fight. Meek little wives feel the edge of the carving knife and study their husbands' necks. Anything can happen. You can even get a full glass of beer at a cocktail lounge.

Just for the fun of it, here's another unforgettable Chandlerism:

> It was a blonde. A blonde to make a bishop kick a hole in a stained glass window.

There's nothing fancy here. The language is unadorned and the sentences are simple. Yet the prose is nuanced, with jokes peeking out from behind the plain-spoken words.

In fantasy, often a more formal voice is used, with the author choosing old-fashioned words and phrases to transport the reader into a different mind-set. Here's an example from *The Golden Compass* by Philip Pullman:

> Lyra and her daemon moved through the darkening hall, taking care to keep to one side, out of sight of the kitchen. The three great tables that ran the length of the hall were laid already, the silver and the glass catching what little light there was, and the long benches were pulled out ready for the guests. Portraits of former Masters hung high up in the gloom along the walls.

Note the longer sentences here that pull the reader through the length of the thought. The construction is more formal, as are the details—darkening hall, silver, portraits of Masters—that make up the voice of the narrator.

A comic story has a lighter, more casual voice, as demonstrated in this excerpt from Christopher Moore's *Bloodsucking Fiends*:

> Sundown painted purple across the great Pyramid while the Emperor enjoyed a steaming whiz against a dumpster in the alley below. A low fog worked its way up from the bay, snaked around columns and over concrete lions to wash against the towers where the West's money was moved. The financial district: an hour ago it ran with rivers of men in gray wool and women in heels; now the streets, built on sunken ships and gold-rush garbage, were deserted—quiet except for a foghorn that lowed across the bay like a lonesome cow.
>
> The Emperor shook his scepter to clear the last few drops, shivered, then zipped up and turned to the royal hounds who waited at his heels. "The foghorn sounds especially sad this evening, don't you think?"

This opening isn't written in Chandler's tough-guy voice because the sentences are longer and the descriptions more elaborate. Moore's voice here is laced with irony. You first get this feeling when you meet "steaming whiz" on the page. Yet the fog leavens the mood; it "snakes." It doesn't roll in, as most fogs are purported to do.

A literary novel evokes a narrative voice that reflects the mood of the story. Here is the voice of Humbert Humbert, infamous narrator of Vladimir Nabokov's *Lolita*:

> Lolita, light of my life, fire of my loins. My sin, my soul. Lo-lee-ta: the tip of the tongue taking a trip of three steps down the palate to tap, at three, on the teeth. Lo. Lee. Ta.
>
> She was Lo, plain Lo, in the morning, standing four feet ten in one sock. She was Lola in slacks. She was Dolly at school. She was Dolores on the dotted line. But in my arms she was always Lolita.

Here, Nabokov conveys a serious voice of a man obsessed with a woman—or in this case, a girl. There's no irony here. No humor. Yet in the first sentence, there is a touch of the lyric.

In *Mount Misery*—a novel infused with a more intellectual and observational irony than Moore or Chandler—Samuel Shem writes with a different voice. Here, as he compares and contrasts human foibles, there's a hint of a sharp blade as he takes a swipe at WASPs.

> Wasps, I'd discovered in my month of being a shrink, are notoriously hard to read. Their body language borders on mute, and their language itself is oblique, like those masters of obliqueness the English who, I had learned in my three years at Oxford, when they say "Yes, actually" mean "No," and when they say "No, actually," may mean anything.

And the voice of a romance novel sets a different mood. Here's an excerpt from Johanna Lindsey's *Love Only Once*:

> 1817 London
>
> The fingers holding the brandy decanter were long and delicate. Selena Eddington was vain about her hands. She showed them off whenever a chance presented itself, as it did just then. She brought the decanter to Nicholas instead of taking his glass to the brandy. This

> served another purpose, as well, for she was able to stand in front of him as he reclined on the plush blue sofa, the fire at her back, her figure outlined provocatively through her thin muslin evening dress. Even a hardened rake like Nicholas Eden could still appreciate a lovely body.

Here, the voice is formal, the sentences longer. There's no irony here. No sly wink. No subtle undertone. Just an erotic come-hither that sets the mood and invites the reader to wonder what happens next.

## NARRATIVE VOICES

Whether the stories are told in first or third person, all of these books are written in a voice that enhances the story—a voice tailor-made for the subject. Each voice is strong and each is unique.

You may have read or been told that first-person voice is easier to individualize than third person. When considering the latter, there's no shortage of advice to writers about how the narrator of a book should disappear, should assume the form of another posy in the flowered fictional wallpaper. Balderdash! Some of the most memorable books you read—the ones that stay with you long after you have closed the covers—have a unique third-person or omniscient narrative voice.

Instead of trying to make the narrator disappear, think of your narrative voice as another character in your book. Some characters like to occupy center stage, others prefer to hang out in the wings. But they all have a distinct and necessary presence. Just as each character speaks in an individual voice, so do you. And the voice you write with will influence how the reader feels about the story.

### Vocal Consistency

In fiction, consistency of voice is critical. You might be ironic one minute and innocent the next, but the reader should be able to depend on your narrative voice remaining essentially the same throughout the book. Indiscriminate mixing and matching—fantasy voice here, Sam Spade voice there—will confuse the reader and most likely cause him to lose interest in your story.

Although this book you're reading and I am writing isn't fiction, it's written in a distinct voice. At least I hope it is. Even though I'm serious in one section, philosophical in another, and—I hope—amusing in another, the voice I use is open and informal. Helpful information mixed with opinion, spiced with humor, seasoned with friendly persuasion, and steeped in the down-home juices of my Oklahoma roots. Come on in. Sit down, make yourself at home. Let's talk about story. And let's have some fun doing it. That's my voice. The one I've chosen to write this book.

But this is not the voice I use in all my books. Each project is different. Each story, fiction or nonfiction, demands its own voice.

I was in Oklahoma City when the Murrah Federal Building was bombed in 1995. In *One April Morning*, the nonfiction book I wrote about the bombing, I maintained a consistent narrative voice throughout the book, then contrasted my own words with the words of children I interviewed. I deliberately chose a more distanced narrative voice so it would stand apart from the poignancy of the children's voices. Their observations served as a Greek chorus—a collective voice—that commented on the action and amplified the more traditional description of the tragedy they had experienced.

> Firefighters and police officers, priests and parents,
> doctors and nurses, friends and strangers,
> rushed to the scene of the blast.
> Wails of sirens drowned out cries for help
> as injured people, dazed and bleeding,
> wandered from the bombed-out buildings.
> Others, less fortunate, were trapped inside.
> At hospitals all over the city, emergency teams assembled to await the arrival of the wounded.
>
> "My mommy was at her hospital," said Gracie.
> "She was looking out for all the people."

"My daddy is a doctor. He went to his hospital," said
   Rachel.
"He waited and waited for someone he could help.
   But nobody came because most of the people were
   dead."
"There were parents walking around outside the build-
   ing with pictures of their kids, asking if anybody had
   seen them," said Brad.

"I was scared," said Melissa, "because my mom was
   downtown."
"I was scared," said Brendon. "My guts were scared and
   I was trying to hide somewhere."

Stronger than a hurricane wind,
louder than crashing thunder,
the helter-skelter bomb blast even blew away
the clothes that people wore.

"My daddy got a two-year-old baby out of the ambulance," said Addi. "It only had socks on."

Because the details of the bombing were familiar to most people
from magazine, television, and newspaper accounts, I needed to
find a different way to tell the story, a way unfamiliar to readers.
In this case, I created two "voices" to play off each other—just
one of many approaches to storytelling.

## Finding Your Voice

Every book has a story. And every story has a voice. Creating
the right interplay between these two elements is critical.

Different projects, different voices. And they're all inside you.
The catch is, in order for you to find your true voice you're going to have to shed your old one. The school voice. The please-
the-teacher voice. And—*horrors!*—the college-term-paper voice.
Allow me to share with you a little anecdote about the latter.

A few years ago I took the exam to enable me to teach in Los
Angeles schools. It probably comes as no surprise that in order to
pass the test, I had to take a brush-up course in math—algebra,

especially. Definitely not my strong suit. Never was. Never will be. I still get a glitch in my stomach when I hear a sentence that begins with, "If a train leaves Chicago traveling at sixty miles an hour ..."

I've never been good at test taking. But other than to refresh my memory about how to structure a formal essay, I didn't worry about the writing portion of the teacher's exam. After all, I'd published thirty-nine books. I didn't need a refresher course in writing.

Big mistake.

Big *big* mistake.

I passed the math portion of the test (a miracle), but I blew the writing. Truth be told, I fell into the "needs work" category, the last stop on the examination line before failure. That's because I had to write three short essays on assigned topics in thirty minutes. Ten minutes per essay. No extra time allowed.

Fifteen minutes into the half hour, I was still trying to formulate what I was going to say, how I was going to approach each topic, which way I was going to express the thoughts, and in what tone and voice I would use to write.

I wanted to say something interesting. Something insightful. Something creative. Perhaps even amusing. And I wanted to say it well.

It never occurred to me in the tangle of creative angst that all the examiners wanted was adequate prose with a well-constructed topic sentence, a couple of supporting statements, and a conclusion. What more can you expect in a ten-minute essay? The judges didn't care if the essay was creative. They didn't care if I used interesting words or presented the material in a unique or memorable way. They just wanted to know I was proficient in the basics of writing, while *I* wanted to know I had created an intriguing essay. In the process of trying to reach my goal, I came perilously close to running out of time and failing the exam.

The fact is, I'd been writing books intended for audiences of children and general readers for years. I had long ago shed my school voice, and it never occurred to me to go back to it.

Other than almost failing the teacher exam, I don't regret for a minute leaving my academic voice in the literary dust. Oh, with a little effort, I suppose I could resurrect the voice with which I wrote term papers in college. The voice that demonstrates good grammar, grasp of subject, and clear use of language—but that has no color, no passion, and no originality.

I could have written this book in this voice:

> In addressing the complex conundrum of the split literary personality, there are two distinct styles the student of writing might choose to emulate. Although the dual options are diametrically opposed, each occupies a valid place within the demanding context of the literary and academic landscape.
>
> One: Learn to write in an efficient and timely manner in whole sentences and adequate prose. Remember to stick in a ten-dollar word every now and then to impress the reader.
>
> Two: Forget the above, invoke your literary muse, and embrace the voice within you.

If you prefer entertainment like this, I recommend *Congressional Quarterly* as an excellent source for light reading.

In other words, before you write for a wider audience, shed your school voice and find a richer, more authentic way to express yourself. Take the time and make the effort to discover the voice that belongs to your story, as well as to *you*—not to your third-grade social studies teacher or your college English professor. Using a voice that comes from the naked core of truth that lives deep inside gives your prose a power and substance that no amount of schooling can create.

Once you discover the authenticity within yourself, you can move into all the other voices that inhabit your imagination with an assurance you never before experienced. This is, after all, the way you honor your essential self and elevate your creative spirit. It is also a way to reclaim the enchantment of mind that is your original nature and your birthright.

## TONE

Beyond the voice you choose to tell the story, you also convey your promise to the reader by the tone—the atmosphere—you create. When you consider the tone of your book, choose your words with care. Consider the rhythm of your sentences, the sound of the language, and the way these elements are combined. Short, terse words and phrases convey an entirely different mood than longer words and sentences.

Are you writing a book that's light and fun to read? Your tone should reflect this. Rebecca Wells achieves this in the first chapter of *Divine Secrets of the Ya-Ya Sisterhood*. The style is Southern casual in which even despair is amusing:

> *Tap-dancing child abuser.* That's what the Sunday *New York Times* from March 8, 1993, had called Vivi. The pages of the week-old Leisure Arts section lay scattered on the floor next to Sidda as she curled up in the bed, covers pulled tightly around her, portable phone on the pillow next to her head.
>
> There had been no sign the theater critic would go for blood. Roberta Lydell had been so chummy, so sisterly-seeming during the interview that Sidda had felt she'd made a new girlfriend ... With subtle finesse, the journalist had lulled Sidda into a cozy false sense of intimacy as she pumped her for personal information.

The tone is light hearted and laced with humor in these opening sentences, starting with "tap-dancing child abuser." The narrator is hurt, surprised. She's been bamboozled by a big-city reporter who reveals that the abuser is Sidda's mother ... a woman enraged by the article.

In *Open Heart*, A.B. Yehoshua's novel of passion and spiritual longing, the author opens his book with the protagonist in the operating room. Here, the tone takes on the feel of surgical precision. Everything is certain, no detail overlooked. This author means business. And yet there is an element of sadness here that we can't avoid noting and wanting to explore.

The incision was ready for stitching now. The anesthetist slipped the mask impatiently from his face, and as if the big respirator with its changing, flickering numbers were no longer enough for him, he stood up, gently took the still hand to feel the living pulse, smiled affectionately at the naked sleeping woman, and winked at me. But I ignored his wink, because my eyes were fixed on Professor Hishin, to see if he would finish the suturing himself or ask one of us to take over. I felt a tremor in my heart. I knew I was going to be passed over again, and my rival, the second resident, was going to be given the job.

In *L.A. Requiem*, Robert Crais's Elvis Cole novel, the tone is macho, tough, and hip. This cop knows the streets. And, from the outset, the reader gets this.

The Islander Palms Motel

Uniformed LAPD Officer Joe Pike could hear the banda music even with the engine idling, the a.c. jacked to meat locker, and the two-way crackling callout codes to other units.

The covey of Latina street kids clumped outside the arcade giggled at him, whispering things to each other that made them flush.

It doesn't take much to establish a distinct tone. In fact, what nails this opening into the reader's mind is the originality of the phrase, "the a.c. jacked to meat locker." Crais doesn't say "the a.c. jacked to the temperature of a meat locker." It's the abbreviated form that packs the punch. A few simple words set the book apart from masses of other novels that strive for a similar effect.

Think of tone as paint. Just as you create different moods in a room when you paint the walls different colors, the language you choose creates different moods in your story. Take advantage of the verbal palate in your command. Your story will be stronger for the effort.

## HOW THE SIBLINGS INTERACT

Voice and tone work together to tell the reader whether your book is a mystery, a romance, a thriller, an historical tale, a time-travel adventure, or a coming-of-age story. Sometimes voice and tone are so interwoven that they seem like identical twins.

In *Moon Women*, Pamela Duncan begins her Southern tale with:

> Ruth Ann wasn't one to cry over nothing, but dang it all if tonight didn't feel worth crying about. A.J. was late coming home again, Angela and Alex had fought all day, the washing machine broke down, she burnt her arm ironing A.J.'s shirts, and to top it all off, she was eight and a half months pregnant with what felt more like a whale than a baby. This kid swam and leaped and butted constantly, grinding against her spine one minute and wringing out her bladder the next. Her whole focus in life had narrowed to survival, counting down to D-day—drop day, dump day, delivery day, thank-you-Jesus-I'll-never-do-that-again-as-long-as-I-live day. Hallelujah!

Duncan uses an amusing voice to create an amusing tone to the story. Here, the two elements blend.

Sometimes, however, voice and tone work at deliberate cross-purposes. In *The Polish Lover*, Anthony Weller uses jazz and irony to drive his bittersweet novel of love and obsession. Throughout the book, the author's voice is cool, deliberately paced—sometimes allegro, sometimes andante, but the prose always maintains a forward momentum with quiet foreshadowing of things to come. And yet there's a subtle elegiac tone here, a sense of regret that fuels the tone with passion.

> Because I am a jazz musician, used to things going wrong, I went to Poland for the holidays.
>
> I am talking about the old Poland, the one you see before you adjust the horizontal hold on the television in your mind: the Poland where people lined up in the cold for two hours just to buy toothpaste or a notepad. I didn't go there to make music, or to learn about

politics. I went with a woman. I'll call her only Maja. If I give her full name—who knows?—some European musicians' union might arrest her and assemble a tribunal of horn players.

I should've been able to resist her, or at least question what we were doing. I am a clarinetist: careful by instinct, classical by training, jazzer by first love. Not everyone realizes the clarinet is the subtlest, most portable and agile reed of all—usually it knows how to look out for itself.

The voice of the narrator is earthbound, matter-of-fact, with just a hint of irony. And yet the tone implies passion as he addresses the reader, basically confessing that he's a fool for love.

Setting tone and voice against each other is a powerful and effective narrative technique. If you want to tell a ghost story, you don't begin with a hero who's a woo-woo kind of guy that already believes in spirits and ghosts. It's more effective to begin with a just-the-facts, ma'am, show-me-or-it-doesn't-exist kind of fellow. And you reflect this attitude in the narrative voice you choose and the way the hero speaks. Short sentences. Strong words. Clear thoughts. After establishing the hero's down-to-earth credentials in the reader's mind, his stunned reaction when he sees the ghost then becomes instantly believable.

How do you accomplish this dual technique? By painting in bold and contrasting colors. You write your story in first or third person and you speak with a no-nonsense, matter-of-fact voice. Then you pull the rug out from under this sensible, rational presentation by creating a threatening situation that evokes uncontrolled passion and fear—remembering always that what you don't see is scarier than what you do. When sibling rivalry is at its peak, the clash is not only dramatic, it's memorable.

## SOME FINAL NOTES

Take the time to experiment with the opening paragraphs of your novel. Just because you've started with one voice or set the stage with one tone doesn't mean you can't try for something more appropriate to your story—something more memorable.

Consider what you can say in one voice that you wouldn't be able to express in another. Nothing locks you into a singular voice except your own decision. Your narrative voice can be dispassionate and distant or it can snuggle up in the reader's imagination and make itself at home. Let your story dictate the choice you make.

Try playing with the tone of your book. Ask yourself what changes in vocabulary would create the transformation you want to make. How can you use contractions to transform the tone? What mental shift must you make to slip into the skin of a character? How does varying the length of the sentences create a soft or a tough tone?

Finally, ask yourself how you could change the voice and tone in your story to make it more compelling.

- Is there a different tone you could use that would make the story stronger?

- Is there a different voice you could use that would make the story more intriguing?

- Is there a way to play voice and tone against each other that would create electricity between the characters?

Don't be afraid to experiment. There's a good chance you could find a more effective way to tell your story and a more vital way to involve the reader.

# 18

# NARRATIVE AUTHORITY

## Setting and Senses

---

*In every piece of fiction ... setting is one
of the three major elements—along with
characterization and plot—that the writer must
weave together to create the narrative.*

—Connie C. Epstein

When I ghostwrote a book a few years ago, the "author" sent me voluminous notes about incidents she wanted included in the book. Time and again I'd open my e-mail and find entries with phrases such as, "I met John William, a filmmaker, and he told me about ..." or "When I sat down to talk with Katherine ..." Again and again I'd write back and ask, "Where and when did you meet him? Who is Katherine and why, where, and when did you talk with her?"

Here, context is everything. Readers hadn't encountered these people before, yet the "author" had given them no anchor in time or place. As a consequence, they couldn't come to life.

An editor friend of mine calls this act of anchoring your story *narrative authority*. By this he means you must give the reader signposts along the way in order to maintain a sense of narrative continuity. Whether you're writing fiction or nonfiction, inserting a character or incident into a story without relating it to the content of the book creates a disconnect with the reader.

It's your job as writer to provide such a vivid context for each of your characters and events that your reader feels like she's participating in the story. In this way, *specificity creates authenticity*.

## THE FIVE Ws

When we were in school, most of us learned the basics of journalism from our teachers. After talking to the class about the assignment at hand, the teacher would turn around and jot five words on the blackboard:

Who?
Where?
When?
What?
Why?

This may be old news, but it's also as current as today's *New York Times* Web site or the novel you are writing.

There are lots of ways to convey this information. You don't need to begin your book with, "It was in Chicago in 1942 that Smasher Malone looked at me one day, curled his fist and gave me a left cross to my jaw—all because he was jealous of me and the girl I took to dinner." Granted, that opening provides answers to all the Ws, but it crams the information into a cramped space. You could use the sentence as a jumping-off point, writing the story as a flashback leading up to the left cross to the jaw. On the other hand, you can mete out the information a little at a time. In fact, you could create an entire novel from the information in that one sentence.

Using this approach, you could string out your information in pieces. Like our old friends Hansel and Gretel dropping crumbs in the forest, you sprinkle the information into your narrative as you tell your story. You needn't sock it to the reader all at once.

Let's look at how to spread out the information from our example.

**Who:** The story begins in graduate school where the twenty-two-year-old narrator named Jonas Chapnick and his best friend, Ted "Smasher" Malone, sit in chemistry class together. They've been friends for two years and now they're both looking at—and desiring—the same girl, as she stands in front of the room to present the paper she has written.

**Where:** Jonas glances out the window of the classroom and notes how dark clouds hang over Lake Michigan and the Chicago skyline.

**When:** After going to a movie on Sunday evening, Jonas and Ted walk outside, pull their coats around them as the icy weather assaults their bodies. On the way home, they hear the newspaper boy crying out. "Extra! Extra! Japanese attack Pearl Harbor!"

Cut to the following day when Jonas sits in front of the radio with his mother, father, and little sister. They listen to President Franklin Roosevelt as he says, "Yesterday, December 7, 1941—a date which will live in infamy—the United States of America was suddenly and deliberately attacked by naval and air forces of the Empire of Japan."

**What:** Two days later we follow Jonas and Ted as they try to enlist in the armed services at the naval recruiting station. As they stand in line, they make a bet about who gets to fight the enemy first.

**Why:** Tension begins to grow between the two young men as they go through boot camp together and wait for the day they are shipped out. Whether it's personal combat or marksmanship, the competition grows between them. When they come home on leave, Jonas asks the object of their mutual affection to dinner before Ted can call her. And thus, the split between the young men is complete.

# SPECIFICITY IN ALL THINGS

As you go through the story of rivalry, conflict, and reconciliation, you anchor each new incident, each new encounter, in time and place. Whether the scene occurs at a diner, on an island in the Pacific, or on the deck of a ship, the reader needs to know where the characters are, what time it is, and how time and place relate to the larger story.

You can begin a paragraph with, "Tuesday evening, Jonas picked up his copy of *A Tale of Two Cities* and settled on his bunk to read" … or you can begin with, "Icy April rain soaked through Ted's windbreaker as he stood watch on the ship." However you choose to anchor the story, readers need to have consistent clues about where the hero is within the overall context of the narrative. Is he at home? At school? What for? When? Why?

## Painting an Enticing Setting

There are lots of things you can do with setting. Setting adds color to the story. Setting affects characters. Setting lends authenticity to the narrative and paints pictures in the imaginations of readers. It's not enough to write about how cold Chicago is in the winter of 1942. You have to *show* us how the cold looks and feels and tastes: Talk about how the icy wind blows off the lake and freezes car-door locks; how icicles hang from the eaves of buildings and snow heaps in soft blankets over cars parked along the streets.

Beyond the weather, facts about the life of the city lend authority to your narrative. Talk about the El, jazz joints, Marshall Fields, the White Sox, soldiers walking along the train tracks in Union Station, duffel bags heaved over their shoulders. These are the details that lend your narrative both credibility and texture.

## Making Sense of Senses

French author Marcel Proust begins his seven-volume novel, *Remembrance of Things Past*, with the narrator of the story sharing tea with his mother and eating small sweet cakes called madeleines. Suddenly the scent of the madeleines transports the storyteller back to the long-forgotten days of his youth. It is sense memory—not conscious recollection—that summons lost scenes from a shrouded past and finally exposes the meaning and significance of the narrator's childhood experience.

Certain "privileged moments" of memory, Proust posits, evoke hidden associations in our unconscious. This, in turn, allows us to exist simultaneously in both past and present—a fleeting transcendence of the limitations of time that permits us a glimpse of the essential truth common to both experiences.

For reader and writer, too, sensory details awaken sleeping thoughts and feelings, allowing our imaginations to exist in two places at once. The sight of a Ford Model T, the texture of velvet, the taste of rock salt, the sound of a jazz riff all create unique and unexpected echoes in our imaginations. Specific sights, sounds, and sensations evoke memories of other times and other places—memories we can use to create stories that move beyond authenticity and into the heart of truth.

Think of your story as a living, organic entity. It breathes, it smells. It touches and it tastes. Your job is to feed these senses, to keep them alive amidst the challenge and conflict and turmoil your hero must confront.

It's not enough to describe how something looks or smells. Take the time to integrate this information with the character.

Instead of writing:

> The pungent scent of the baking bread penetrated the house.

Consider:

> The pungent scent of the baking bread penetrated the dusky corners of the house, reminding Marianne she hadn't eaten since morning.

This kind of sensory detail not only describes the smell of the bread, it establishes the time of day and invites the reader into the mind and body of the hero of the story.

## Exploring the Five Senses

Most of us are fortunate enough to be born with our five senses intact. Throughout our lives, our experience feeds these senses. We develop likes and dislikes. We avoid some things, embrace others. Our senses enrich us at the same time they inform us.

When you write, keep all of these senses in mind. Here is a list of things to trigger your own memories, to use as springboards for the sensory details you integrate into your own book. Add items to the list. Delete others. Tweak it, edit it, enhance it. Make the list your own.

### Smell
baking bread
car exhaust
chile pepper
eucalyptus
fish
incense
laundry detergent
lemon
mint
puppies
roast beef cooking
roses
sea breezes
smoke
sneezy smells
wood-burning fire

### Sound
ambulance siren
baby's cry
Bach
chalk on a blackboard
children playing
chimes
cicadas
hymns

kitten's meow
mother's voice
ocean waves
rain on the roof
tenors
thunder
trumpets
water flowing from the tap
whispers
wind in the trees

## Sight

babies
birthday cake
blue eyes
bumper-to-bumper traffic
cartoon page
Christmas tree
father's face
garbage dump
IRS notice
mountains
new bike
ocean waves
puppies
red sports car
sailboat
sunsets

## Touch

buzz cut
caterpillar crawling on finger
cold water
concrete wall
feathers
hair
hot stove
muscles

new book
orange rind
sandpaper
shag carpet
silk and satin
skateboard
soda can
soil
wooden banister
worn velour of old teddy bear

### Taste and Texture
bitter (arugula, cranberries, horseradish)
chewy (roast beef, gum, mozzarella)
crunchy (cashews, carrots, toast)
hot (cinnamon, chilies, garlic)
mushy (beans, mashed potatoes, liver)
salty (peanuts, chicken soup, potato chips)
sour (lemon, lime)
sweet (brownies, ice cream, nectarines)

## The Devil's in the Details

It is possible to create too much of a good thing. Too much detail can destroy your story. Seven years ago I edited a book that took place in America at the turn of the twentieth century. It was obvious the author had done massive amounts of research in order to create a story that was authentic to time and place. Every last iota of information the writer knew about this historical period was integrated into the book. The deluge of architectural detail, cultural facts, thoughts, quotes, history, customs, and costumes from the period drowned what was essentially an intriguing and well-plotted story.

If yours is a book that has required lots of research, make certain your story doesn't take a back seat to the facts and figures you include. Otherwise your narrative threads will be overwhelmed by details and your story will be lost along with your reader.

My point: *Just because you have done massive amounts of research doesn't mean you should include it all in your book.*

Take some consolation in that fact that when you make the effort to do your research in order to be historically and culturally accurate, your time is never lost. Readers appreciate the details you do include. And even if you don't use everything you've learned, the knowledge you've accumulated allows you to write with an authority and authenticity you could not otherwise convey. When it comes to research, treat it like salt. Use only what is necessary and set aside the rest.

# 19

# THE WRITE WAY

## The Finer Points of Good Writing

---

*When you catch an adjective, kill it.*

—Mark Twain

When I first began to write, I thought adjectives and adverbs were honestly and truly fabulous, entrancing and enhancing. My overblown prose was virtually littered with these pesky, annoying parts of speech. It took me a long time to figure out that adjectives interfere with prose more often than they improve it and adverbs kill a sentence more often than they enliven it.

Some people are born with an understanding of strong writing. They feel the rhythm and hear the music from the moment they set pen to paper. Most of us, however, aren't blessed with this natural gift. We lesser mortals must learn how to write—must practice our art and hone our craft as part of our daily discipline.

It took me fifteen years to learn how to write. What a waste. I know now that it's not necessary to squander a major chunk of your productive literary life hacking a path through a jungle of words in search of powerful prose. There's another way to master the craft. In this chapter, I'll share with you what took me a decade and a half to learn.

## TWENTY-FIVE RULES FOR GOOD WRITING

Strong prose is a matter of practice and discipline and conscious awareness of the words you put on the page. There are rules for effective writing, and you can save yourself a lot of unnecessary grief if you take the time to incorporate them into your writing psyche.

These rules can't make a good writer a brilliant one. But they can make an average writer a good writer, and a good writer a better writer. They can also turn a mediocre story into a memorable one.

### I. Never Let the Truth Get in the Way of Your Story
Creative writing is just that: creative. If the truth prevents you from telling your fictional story effectively, get rid of the facts and invent something that makes the story work.

### 2. Show, Don't Tell
This is one of the most basic rules of storytelling. Don't tell me how someone feels. Show me.

Instead of:

> The vampire was thrilled when he saw he was standing near the entrance to the blood bank.

Write:

> When the vampire read the sign that said Blood Bank, he grinned and licked his lips.

### 3. Never Use Two Words When One Word Will Do
Less is more. Usually one powerful word will do the same job as two weaker ones.

Instead of:

> Andrea stared at the horrible, slithering mass
> of snakes.

Write:

> Andrea stared at the writhing mass of snakes.

## 4. Use the Active Voice

The difference between adequate prose and good prose is the difference between the passive and active voice. Make certain that active verbs drive your prose.

Instead of:

> There were a great number of dead bodies on
> the ground.

Write:

> Dead bodies littered the ground.

## 5. Use Parallel Construction

Parallel construction allows you to write in the most interesting, economical fashion by aligning your verb tenses and uniting phrases with a common construction.

Instead of:

> The Vampire bared his teeth and then, raising
> his claws to sharpen them, he started licking his
> chops. "Gotcha!" he said with a grin.

Write:

> The Vampire bared his teeth, sharpened his
> claws, and licked his chops. "Gotcha!" he said
> with a grin.

## 6. Keep Related Words Together

Linguistic studies have shown that most of us have a natural instinct for the placement of adjectives. We don't say, "I have a blue shiny car." Instead, we say, "I have a shiny blue car." The same principle should be applied to the sentences you write.

Instead of:

> Frankenstein noticed a large bloodstain in the rug that
> was in the middle.

Write:

> Frankenstein noticed a large bloodstain in the middle
> of the rug.

## 7. Replace Adjectives and Adverbs With Vivid Nouns and Active Verbs

Cultivate the use of strong verbs and concrete nouns. They are the most powerful tools in a writer's arsenal.

Instead of:

> Since the day Barbara met the werewolf, she felt very
> scared and frightened.

Write:

> Since the day she met the werewolf, terror haunted
> Barbara's heart.

There is no surer way to weaken your prose than to pepper it with adverbs. In fact, adverbs are so loathed by professional writers, I heard of a poetry teacher in Los Angeles who insists his students contribute five dollars to the class party fund for every adverb they use.

There are, of course, times when the adverb is appropriate and necessary. Choose those times carefully.

> She looked longingly and lovingly at the chocolate.

Or

> She looked at the chocolate with longing and love.

Or better

> Her eyes consumed the chocolate.

## 8. Avoid Qualifiers and Other Wimpy Words

What are these words that blunt meaning and weaken prose? Rather, a lot, almost, sort of, about, somewhat, little, feel, big, pretty, just, maybe, beautiful, nice, extremely, partially, and very. One small word can make a big difference. This point is related to tip no. 7. If you have to use a qualifier, you aren't using the best possible noun or verb. State the fact. Don't equivocate. Don't dilute.

Instead of:

> The teacher was very angry and dismayed when she read the report.

Write:

> The teacher was angry and dismayed when she read the report.

## 9. Avoid Purple Prose

Create a graveyard for all those once-beloved adverbs and adjectives. Save the strong words and bury the rest. Purple prose isn't more descriptive for readers, it's just more distracting.

Instead of:

> Tiffany Cerise smiled prettily, her beautiful, enticing, cat-green eyes dancing seductively with alluring and predatory fires.

Write:

> When Tiffany smiled, her eyes danced with predatory fires.

## 10. Don't Overexplain

Give your reader the benefit of the doubt and allow him to intuit the meaning of the dialogue, rather than read about it.

Instead of:

> "I'm sorry," Peter said consolingly.

Write:

> "I'm sorry," Peter said.

## 11. Eliminate All Unnecessary Uses of *That*

This is a trick that simplifies your construction and cleans up your prose.

Instead of:

> Eliminate all the uses of that that you possibly can.

Write:

> Eliminate all the uses of that you possibly can.

## 12. Use Short Paragraphs When Possible

> Long paragraphs exhaust the eye and intimidate the reader. Short paragraphs help maintain a reader's focus.

## 13. Write Cinematically

When you write, think visually. Language offers endless possibilities for a creative approach to expressing an idea.

Eddy Peters exemplified this when he wrote, "Not only does the English Language borrow words from other languages, it sometimes chases them down dark alleys, hits them over the head, and goes through their pockets." (P.S. Note the parallel construction.)

## 14. Vary Your Sentence Structure

Using nothing but noun–verb declarative sentences makes for dull reading. Break up the monotony.

Instead of:

> John walked to the closet. He opened the door. He took one look inside and he screamed.

Write:

> John walked to the closet and opened the door. Taking one look inside, he screamed.

## 15. Use Interesting Contrasts

Search for ways to combine things that don't belong together—
like the owl on the beach from chapter two. Readers loved Vito
Corleone because he was both a scoundrel and a hero.

## 16. Juxtapose Words and Ideas to
## Evoke Humor and Irony

As you write, look for opportunities to play with words and
combine unlikely ideas.

> I believe in the kindness of strangers and the
> existence of evil.

And

> The class president is a kid who lurches before
> he leaps.

## 17. Create Interest by Mixing Ideas

Mixing alien ideas and drawing unlikely parallels will make
the writing fresh. This also keeps your writing from falling
into cliché.

> She was the kind of girl who collected men like
> she collected speeding tickets. They both hap-
> pened when she wasn't paying attention.

## 18. Avoid Highfalutin' Words

Don't use a ten-dollar word when a five-dollar word will do.
Big words don't make your prose sound more intelligent; they
make it sound pretentious and unprofessional.

*Utilize* or *use, transpire* or *happen, automobile* or *car*—choose
the simple word.

## 19. Listen to the Music of the Words

Just as in poetry, the best prose has a rhythm to it. Honor that
rhythm. There have been days when I've spent half an hour
searching the thesaurus for a word that has three syllables instead

of two. Sometimes the difference is subtle, but it can make the reading experience more satisfying.

Instead of:

> Some writers catch onto the rhythm and they delight in the sound of the music as soon as they learn to write.

Write:

> Some writers feel the rhythm and hear the music from the moment they learn to write.

## 20. Watch Out for Word Repetition

There's nothing more tiresome for a reader than seeing the same tiresome words over and over in the same paragraph. This creates the overall impression the reader is reading the same repetitive, tiresome prose over again and it tires out the reader.

Note: The exception to this rule—the critical exception—is when you repeat a word for emphasis.

## 21. Beware of *It*

Grammarians call *it* an "obscure pronominal reference." That's when *it* is left dangling in a sentence without a clear reference to whom or what it refers. Your reader should be able to follow it without having to reread it in an effort to figure out what it is saying or referring to. Got it?

So double-check your sentences for dangling *it*s.

Where you find:

> Kathy couldn't believe it was happening.

Clarify:

> Kathy couldn't believe her sister was finally accepting the blame.

## 22. Write Sentences in the Positive Form

Cast your sentences in the positive, rather than the negative.

Borrowing from *The Elements of Style* by William Strunk Jr. and E.B. White, instead of:

> When it came to appointments, she was not a prompt person.

Write:

> She was chronically late to her appointments.

Some other examples:

> Not honest vs. dishonest
>
> Not important vs. trifling
>
> Did not remember vs. forgot
>
> Did not pay attention vs. ignored
>
> Did not have much confidence in vs. distrusted

## 23. Learn to Use, Not Abuse, Metaphor and Simile

Metaphor and simile are similar, in that they both delineate comparisons between unlike things.

To quote Constance Hale, from her book *Sin and Syntax*, "In metaphor the comparison is expressed when a figurative term is substituted for a literal term."

When Shakespeare says, "All the world's a stage," he is using metaphor.

In simile, the comparison is expressed with words such as *like, as,* and *similar to.*

When Robert Burns says, "O, my Love is like a red, red rose," he is using simile.

Both of these literary devices lend power and substance to your writing. If you overuse them, however, they will dilute that same writing.

## 24. Write. Rewrite. Rewrite

Before:

> There are transcendent moments in a writer's life when a paragraph or a page she or he writes is perfect the first time it is written. Trust me: These moments

are as rare as rain in the Sahara. Most well-regarded
prose is rewritten, reworked, and re-edited.

After:

There are transcendent moments in a writer's life when
a paragraph or page is perfect the first time it is written.
These moments are rare as rain in the Sahara. Most
strong prose is rewritten, reworked, and re-edited.

## 25. There's an Exception to Every Rule

Just because I write in absolutes and sound as if I know what
I'm talking about doesn't mean these rules are carved in stone.
What it does mean is I'm right 93.7 percent of the time. The
other 6.3 percent falls under the rubric of exception to the rule.
Your job is to learn to tell which is which by reading good prose,
practicing your writing, and increasing your awareness.

## EDITORIAL PET PEEVES

In order to avoid annoying some overworked editor with usage
errors and grammatical gaffes—or worse, giving her an excuse
to turn down your manuscript—here are some language fundamentals every writer should know. Pay attention to them.
These nit-picking points can define the distinction between
professional and amateur writing.

I hasten to add that the following peeves are just the tip of
the verbal boo-boo iceberg. Every writer should make the effort
to use clear, concise language that honors words and meanings
by using them correctly.

### Top Ten Rules of Verbal Combat

#### *1. Alright vs. All Right*
When I was in seventh grade, my teacher, Albert E. Stone
(later Professor of American Studies at Emory University and
the University of Iowa), told us that if we misspelled "all right,"

we would pay for our errant ways. A month later, one of my essays was returned with a hole in the page and a note from Mr. Stone: "The next time you misspell this word, there will be nothing left of your essay except the margin." I learned my lesson. And so in spite of some notables who've been known to misspell the word, I insist that it is not all right to spell *all right* "alright."

## 2. Less vs. Few
*Less* refers to quality, *few* refers to quantity.

> There is less frost on the pumpkins this year, but there are fewer pumpkins in the patch.

Or as one grammatically correct grocery chain says, "10 items or fewer."

## 3. Presently vs. Currently
*Presently* means in a little while. *Currently* means now. Presently never means currently.

> The president is currently busy, but he will be with you presently.

## 4. Loan vs. Lend
*Loan* is a noun, *lend* is a verb.

> Mary told Bert she would be happy to lend him the money to pay his loan.

## 5. Me vs. I
*Me* and *I* are both pronouns. *I* is always a subject, *me* is always an object.

> The prize money was sent to my dog and me. It was never never never sent to my dog and I. Furthermore, this secret windfall must remain between you and me—never between you and I. You and I belong at the beginning of a sentence.

An easy way to remember this is to take out the other person and rephrase the sentence. "The money was sent to I" sounds wrong. So does "between I and you."

## 6. He/She vs. Him/Her

Just as in *Me vs. I*, there are lots of writers and speakers who confuse these words—including George W. Bush, who said, "You teach a child to read, and he or her will be able to pass the literary test."

To clarify: *He* and *she* are pronouns. *Him* and *her* are used as objects of a verb or a preposition.

> Simon gave the book to him and her. He would never give the book to she and he. Nor would Simon give the book to he and I, or she and I.

Simon would, however, give the book to her and me, or him and me.

Furthermore, him and I don't go to the movies. Her and he don't hold hands in the movies. Nor do he and her do anything anywhere anyhow. But she and he and I can do anything we want.

## 7. Among vs. Between

Generally speaking, *between* is used when referring to two objects or people; *among* is used when referring to more than two.

> Since the choice is between good and evil, I needn't wander among the other behavioral shades of gray.

## 8. Each Other vs. One Another

Although lots of reputable writers break this rule, *each other* generally refers to two people, *one another* to more than two.

> The twins torment each other constantly. The quadruplets get along with one another most of the time.

## 9. Lie vs. Lay

This one's a biggie—a peeve that ranks high on my personal list. To wit: *Lie, lay,* and *lain* are intransitive verbs. They take no object. *Lay, laid,* and *laid* (yes, *laid* is used for two different tenses) are transitive verbs that take an object. In other words, chickens lay eggs (the objects), people do not.

> Today I lie on the beach. Yesterday I lay on the beach. I also have lain on the beach.

> Today I lay the book on the table. Yesterday I laid the book on the table. I also have laid the book on the table.

> I never never **never** lay on the beach or the couch or the bed or the floor—or anywhere else, for that matter. I don't lie the book on the table, either.

## 10. Farther vs. Further

*Farther* refers to distance. *Further* refers to time or quantity.

> I can throw the ball farther than you. But you can pursue this contest further if you wish.

## Final Note

There are scads of fine points about style and usage that should be mastered by anyone who is serious about writing. And there are scads of books written about this subject. I'm still a student of language and I always will be. I learn new stuff all the time.

For a basic understanding of constructing prose, however, I suggest you invest in a copy of William Strunk Jr. and E.B. White's *The Elements of Style.* This book was first published by Strunk in 1918. It's been revised over the years to keep up with the times, but it is still the high holy bible of writing and style.

For a hip, contemporary guide to language and writing, read Constance Hale's *Sin and Syntax: How to Craft Wickedly Effective Prose.* Hale's humor and intelligence are marvels of wisdom and common sense. Her text will make better a writer of anyone who reads it.

Both of these books amuse while they instruct, and both are worth reading. As a writer, you should refer to them often.

## TEAR AND COMPARE

Take the opening chapter of the book you're writing. Go through it sentence by sentence and apply the Twenty-Five Rules for Good Writing to your own prose. Indulge me: Do this even if you disagree with some of the rules and you think I'm full of baloney.

Once you've changed the chapter, compare the old version with the new.

Ask yourself which one is stronger.

If you belong to a writer's critique group or have writer friends who are willing to read your pages, show the chapter to them. Ask them which version they prefer.

Finally, apply what you've learned to the rest of your book.

PART V

# FINISHING TOUCHES

## 20

# COMING UNGLUED

## Dealing With Writer's Block

---

*It often seems to me that the biggest single issue
for a writer is how to stay buoyant enough to go
on writing. How not to drown.*

—Janette Turner Hospital

In writing, there are moments when our confidence disappears and our courage fades—when staying afloat is all we can manage. This loss of heart can happen to the strongest soul. Nobody is immune to the crisis of faith. Nobody is exempt from the confrontation with failure.

William Butler Yeats describes this agony of mind in his poem, "The Second Coming": "Things fall apart; the centre cannot hold;/Mere anarchy is loosed upon the world." Our world.

For writers, this crisis often comes in the form of an inability to put words on the page. Some people call it writer's block. Some people look the other way and pretend they don't see the elephant in the room. Others immerse themselves in organizing their files or cleaning their closets—or, like me, they indulge in creative procrastination. There is always another errand to run, an appointment to keep, a bill to pay, a weed to pull, or an opportunity to play ball with my dog.

If you haven't yet reached this crisis point in your writing career, be grateful. If it ever does happen, know there is something you can do about it.

# THE BIG UGLY

I don't want to dwell on this subject at length. The superstitious part of me doesn't want to invest too much power in this state of mind. But I do want to offer some practical suggestions should you ever find yourself stuck in this bad place.

## Eight Tips to Find Your Way Back to Your Book

**1. Make a list of reasons why you love the story.** Why is this story worth writing? What makes the hero special? How does this story speak to you? How does it speak to your audience? Whose life will this story touch? What is it about the story that made you want to write it in the first place?

**2. Skip the section that's giving you trouble and write a different part of the book.** Who says you have to write a book in order from beginning to end? You know how the story begins. There's a good chance you know how it ends. If you're stuck in the beginning, skip to the middle or the end. If you're stuck in the middle, skip to the end. Wait until later to fill in the gaps.

**3. Put the book away for ten days.** "Forget" about the book. No matter how much you want to look at the manuscript, don't touch it. Don't even peek. Let the book float in your unconscious while you go to work, take walks, ride your bike, indulge in creative naps, or catch up on all the chores you've been neglecting. Then return to the story refreshed. It's amazing how much perspective distance gives you.

**4. Keep a daily journal about the book.** Spend three days *not* working on the book. Instead, make notes in a journal on characters and plot points. Write down ideas. Explore new ways to express your premise and themes. Take the Zen approach: Don't force the book. Open yourself to the story. Allow the story to flower.

**5. Get feedback from other writers.** Find a writer's group to join. Or hire an editor or writing coach to help you with your book. New points of view can help you get unstuck. Whether in person or online, a solid critique from other writers or editors can open up your vision and expand your storytelling horizons. These people can also help you solve character and plot problems that stand in the way of your story.

**6. Embrace solitude.** There is comfort in being alone. There is renewal in retreat. Sometimes the answer to your problem lies not in the well-meaning opinions and advice of other writers, but within yourself. Try to get away—be it to a cabin in the woods or behind a closed door in your own house—and refill the cup. This is how a writer comes home.

**7. Listen to the silence.** We all have voices that must be heeded, voices that must be heard. Not the negative voices that tell us what we cannot do, but the voices that tell us what we can do—that speak to us of our stories and our characters and our lives.

We cannot hear these voices if we fill our lives with noise.

Listen.

Listen to the silence.

**8. Write.** Write anything. Writing enforces will. Write grocery lists or journal entries or essays. If you can't manage that, make lists of words. Favorite words. Angry words. Happy words. Silly words. Splendid words. Power words. If you can't write anything at all, copy. Copy the opening paragraphs of your favorite books. Copy until you can write again: one line, two lines, one short sentence at a time. Write. Always write.

## AFTERTHOUGHT

If you are stuck, focus on the immutable fact that nothing—neither darkness nor light, neither sorrow nor joy—ever remains the same. Remind yourself that there are times in all our lives when we lose our daring, when we lose our nerve. There are times when we live in fear of being found out, when putting words on the page is impossible. There are also times when we must wander in the wilderness in order to save ourselves. But this malady called writer's block is often no more than a momentary loss of will. Time repairs some things; determination restores others. Whatever the cause for your temporary lapse, there is a cure.

Patience. Intent. Tenacity. Fortitude. Spirit. Faith. Forgiveness. These qualities illuminate the dark times and accentuate the light.

Believe.

# THE CREATIVE SPIRIT
## The Care and Feeding of Your Muse

*Writing is something you do alone in a room. ...*
*The only thing you really need ... is the talent*
*of the room. Unless you have that, your other*
*talents are worthless.*

—Michael Ventura

Most people think creativity is a mystery. You either have it or you don't. That's nonsense—utter nonsense. Creativity is the gift that lifts us out of the ether and makes us human. The problem is, from early childhood, most of us are taught that imagination is inferior to intellect ... that creativity is inferior to logic. And thus, bit by bit, we get our inventiveness and our vision "civilized" out of us.

Creativity is a voracious animal. It needs to be fed regularly. If you leave it untended for too long, you run the risk of starving your passion and diminishing your spirit. Since society tends to value conformity over creativity, this is easy enough to do. Few people will notice the loss.

One night, when my niece Carolyn was three years old, she pointed to a wispy cloud drifting over the moon and exclaimed, "Look, Grandma! The moon is melting!"

Because the realities of life had not yet inhibited the purity of her imagination, that sweet child's vision was as luminous and fanciful as a poet's. Creativity is part of our essential nature. It is our birthright, a blessing connected with the most fundamental core of our being. And as such, it should be kindled and honored, and treated not only with kindness but also respect.

# NINE WAYS TO NOURISH THE CREATIVE SPIRIT

## I. Read, Read, Read

For a writer, reading is the food that sustains the discipline. Read books, fiction and nonfiction. Read poetry and magazines and newspapers. Read everything.

However, it isn't enough merely to read. When I first began to write, I thought my lifetime of reading would sustain me in my novice efforts. The problem was, I had never approached reading with a consciousness of what the writer was doing; I'd never noticed the technique behind the fiction. Therefore, when I began to construct my own story, I didn't know how to do it.

If you want to learn how to write, you need to learn how to read in a way that will teach you how to write. Awareness is the key.

### Questions to ask yourself as you read

- How does the author open the story?
- How does the author handle a shift in time?
- How does the author move from one place to another?
- How does the author introduce the hero?
- How are plot and subplot woven together?

- How does the hero change and evolve from beginning to end?
- How is the villain portrayed?
- How does the author create tension?
- What are the obstacles the hero must overcome?
- How does the author open different scenes?
- How are questions posed and curiosity maintained?
- What is the throughline of the book?
- How does language enhance the story?
- How are the voices of the characters differentiated?
- How does the author convey the tone of the story?
- What propels the story from beginning to middle to end?
- Why is the ending inevitable?

## 2. Explore the Arts

Art is not born in a vacuum. Movies, plays, art exhibits, concerts, all these events are drawn from the common well of creativity. Not only do they enrich one another, they improve one another.

Experiencing the creative output of others opens our minds and our vision to new worlds. Note how an abstract painting by Mark Rothko speaks to us about longing and spirituality. Whether it is a play about a dying parent, a film about a disaffected youth, or a symphony about a heroic leader, the creative core of all art can teach us about the creative spirit in our own lives.

## 3. Heed the Three Ds

Writing isn't a matter of sitting around and waiting for the spirit to move you. Writing requires desire, discipline, and determination. That's not always easy when you have a full-time job or family problems, or you're a parent struggling to make ends meet. But that's when you need the three Ds most.

### Desire

Most of us can't simply toss off a book and expect it to sell. You not only have to entertain the notion of writing a book, you have to *want* to write it—to be willing and enthusiastic about committing the time it takes to see the project through completion.

You have to want it enough to back up desire with discipline and determination.

## Discipline

Discipline means sitting at the desk every day. Whether you are in the mood to write or not, whether you don't feel well, or you're stuck, or you have family obligations, you must write anyway. This means that you honor your art by honing your craft. Discipline means you make up your mind not to let yourself down.

## Determination

When you're determined to do something, you learn not to let obstacles bring you to a stop. This isn't to say the best laid plans don't sometimes go awry. We've all been waylaid by life. Part of determination means opening yourself to the experience and learning how to roll with the punches.

## My 3-D day

I began my first novel when my sons were six and eight years old. We lived in a small cottage, and the only place I had to write was a tiny table set near the back door where neighborhood children ran in and out of the house all day long.

I started writing the novel in the fall. By spring I had moved into the heart of the book and momentum was on my side. I was stoked, I was cooking, I was running on all cylinders.

One fine October morning, I discovered both my boys had developed a condition that required that I wash every item in the house they or we had touched. Sheets, towels, clothes—everything that could be washed should be washed.

Between kids running back and forth past my desk, between fixing lunch and cleaning the kitchen, between washing, folding, and putting away seven loads of laundry, between supervising children all day long, I pounded out twenty pages on my Smith Corona portable.

On a good day with no interruptions, twenty pages would be a spectacular accomplishment. On this day, it was a miracle. I can only tell you I did it because I was driven by the three Ds I am now writing about—thirty years and forty-three books later.

## 4. Set Goals

Successful writers set goals for themselves. Once they set those goals, they do everything in their power to stick to them. The discipline to achieve those goals is essential to the creative process.

### *Time goals*

Some writers decide on a specific amount of time they're going to spend writing each day. Whether they can only manage half an hour or are able to devote eight hours a day to their craft as Dr. Seuss did, they sit themselves down at their desk and stay there until that goal has been met.

This doesn't mean every moment of that time is devoted exclusively to writing. But the daily discipline of being there sets the standard for your craft.

### *Page goals*

If time spent at the desk doesn't feel right for you, set a minimum number of words or pages to write per day. Whether it's one or five or ten pages a day, set your goal and stick to it, no matter what.

Writing a book brings out the restlessness in me. I get up and down from the desk a lot. I walk into the garden and check the flowers, deadhead the pansies, count the number of caterpillars munching on my fennel. I go on errands, talk to friends, and walk my dog. As a consequence, a time goal isn't effective for me.

When I'm writing a book, I set my minimum at five pages a day. This means whether I'm in the mood or not; whether I produce five pages and use every word, or produce five pages and throw every word away the next day, I must turn out those pages. No matter how late the hour or how exhausted I am, I don't leave the desk for the day until I have accomplished this goal.

## 5. Embrace the Process

I often look at writing as a schizophrenic process. One part of me focuses on the goal, the other part focuses on where I am at any given moment.

I'm blessed. Even though I wrestle with prose, I love my work. I love the process of writing, the sound, the rhythm, the taste and texture of language. I love the way words roll around in my mind until they find their way home. Not all writers feel this way. As Red Smith once said, "Writing is easy. I just open a vein and bleed."

Whether you enjoy the process of writing or not, my advice is to make your peace with it. It is the process—not the goal—that gets you where you want to go.

## 6. Honor the Mystery and Magic

Whatever some people might say, there is a mystery to writing. There is magic. Not in how we get our creativity, but how we use it. There is an element of surprise—of ideas appearing out of nowhere and connections leaping out of dreams—that cannot be accounted for in the daily living of our lives. Call it woo-woo. Call it inspiration. Call it synthesis. Call it whatever you wish. This magical and mysterious element of the creative process does exist. To ignore it is to put your book and your creative life at risk.

## 7. Seek the Universal

The reason certain books resonate with readers is because they touch on universal themes. But these themes are not created at a universal level. They are grounded in the particular experience of a particular person at a particular moment in time.

The appeal of most literary heroes—whether they are in fiction or in nonfiction—is that they touch on our innate relationship with sadness or joy or loss. They illuminate how we celebrate and how we deal with personal demons. And they also invite us to consider who we are and who we wish we could be.

## 8. Daydream

As children, most of us were admonished to pay attention to the task at hand and—for goodness sake—stop daydreaming! What a disservice this message conveys to children. Vision and fantasy, creativity and imagination live at the heart of daydreams. They are gifts to be welcomed, not dismissed.

So take a deep breath and open yourself up to the magic.

## 9. Dare

Experiment. Combine unexpected elements. Play with words. Break the rules. Seek out the laughter in desperation and the pain in humor. Writing is a risk. Take the dare.

# MUSINGS ABOUT THE MUSE

In Greek mythology, the traditional Muses are the nine daughters of Zeus that preside over the arts and sciences. (The Greeks also honored three earlier Muses dedicated to Meditation, Remembrance, and Song.) In my personal mythology, I believe we are all born with a Muse. And it is our responsibility to nurture this gift. The problem is, most of us have it "civilized" out of us before the age of seven. Either that, or we ignore this gift for so long that it dies of disinterest and neglect.

We all struggle to achieve a measure of worldly success. But in the process of this struggle, many of us forget how to honor the creative force within.

Some people invoke this part of themselves through prayer. Others by meditation. Others reach this goal through becoming involved in an absorbing activity such as running, gardening, sewing, cooking, tai chi, or carpentry. However you get there, welcome the fanciful and the unusual into your life by continuing to seek new ways to elevate your spirit and celebrate your imagination.

## The Care and Feeding of the Muse

In case all this Muse talk is making you nervous, I'll up the woo-woo ante and add the following instructions.

### Don't mess with the Muse

Don't delude yourself: You need the Muse more than she needs you. Therefore, if your Muse appears to have gone on vacation, I suggest persuasion instead of threats. Entice her into your life with gentle exercises. Close your eyes. Breathe deeply. Meditate. Daydream. Pray.

### Never take the Muse for granted

Unconditional love isn't part of the spiritual vocabulary of the Muse. Just because you've been cruising down the creative highway on automatic pilot, don't assume the Muse will always be riding shotgun. The Muse is temperamental. She's cranky. Like any other being, she needs to be acknowledged regularly. If you don't pay attention to her, she's likely to jump out of the car the next time you come to a stoplight.

### Trust the Muse

Believe. It's not always easy to trust the path that's been laid out before you. Even though you're filled with fear, if your calling is to write, honor that calling. Creative courage isn't won over-night, but the prize is worth the effort.

### Thank the Muse

Thank your Muse for being there for you every day, inspiring your creativity. You express your gratitude by staying open to the creative leap; by meditating and remembering; by being receptive to new ideas and welcoming fresh ways of thinking.

# ⟿ AFTERWORD ⟾

*Nothing in the world can take the place of persistence.
Talent will not; nothing is more common than
unsuccessful men with talent. Genius will not;
unrecorded genius is almost a proverb. Education will
not; the world is full of educated derelicts. Persistence
and determination alone are omnipotent.*

—Calvin Coolidge

We all walk the wire when we sit down in front of a blank page or an empty computer screen. We all work without a net. Sometimes it's hard to find our balance. Sometimes it's hard to recover from a fall. Sometimes it's hard to bear the loneliness or disappointment. And sometimes it's hard to find the strength to begin or the courage to believe. But with attention and focus and determination, it is possible for us to complete that long and scary journey to the other side.

How do we do this? One foot in front of another. One step at a time.

One word in front of another.

One sentence at a time.

Here.

Now.

Take a deep breath.

Step off the edge.

And begin.

## READING LIST
### Resources for Writers

Whether you're a novice or a published author, reading books about writing can open up new worlds and give rise to new ideas. These books can also offer you comfort when you're stuck and show you new ways to approach old problems.

Sometimes you need a plain how-to book. Other times you need philosophical insight to the craft. Whatever your preference, you'll find it on this list.

*Bird by Bird* by Anne Lamott

*The Writing Life* by Annie Dillard

*Scene & Structure* by Jack M. Bickham

*How to Write a Damn Good Novel* by James N. Frey

*How to Write a Damn Good Novel II* by James N. Frey

*Sin and Syntax: How to Craft Wickedly Effective Prose* by Constance Hale

$\mathcal{Clee}$ APPENDIX $\mathcal{Crelle}$

# GENRES AND SUBGENRES
## (Supplement to Chapter Three)

---

As I compiled this list to accompany the genres I presented in chapter three, I wondered how many of the titles I'd chosen had garnered prizes, been made into movies, or been the genesis of other works. Frankly, I was astonished at the number of iterations and transformations some of the books had enjoyed—not to mention the prizes they'd won. All of these stories offer depths of character and plot that novelists, filmmakers, and playwrights can mine to capture the imaginations of their audience.

**Full Disclosure:** The list of titles in this appendix is not carved in stone. Readers will certainly find ample reason to disagree with at least some of the subgenres and titles. The compilation is, by necessity, limited, so no doubt you'll come up with your own additions. Nevertheless, this list—an eclectic mix of the classic and contemporary—offers some books to help you examine and understand the demands of the genre you're aiming for.

## GENERAL FICTION
Chick Lit *(diaries, etc., for the girls)*
> *Bridget Jones's Diary* by Helen Fielding
> *Diary of a South Beach Party Girl* by Gwen Cooper
> *The Nanny Diaries* by Emma McLaughlin and Nicola Kraus

## Domestic Drama *(life from comedy to tragedy)*

*Shadow Ranch* by Jo-Ann Mapson

*Girls in Trouble* by Caroline Leavitt

*The Prince of Tides* by Pat Conroy

## Sports *(variations on the Roman circus)*

*Waggle* by Joe Redden Tigan

*Shoeless Joe* by W.P. Kinsella

*North Dallas Forty* by Peter Gent

## Vampire Lit *(ouch! that hurts)*

*Dracula* by Bram Stoker

*Interview With the Vampire* by Anne Rice

*Baltimore, or, The Steadfast Tin Soldier and the Vampire* by Mike Mignola and Christopher Golden

## LGBT Lit *(life, love, and romance)*

*Tales of the City* by Armistead Maupin

*Edinburgh* by Alexander Chee (Asian Writer's Workshop prize; Michener/Copernicus Prize; Lambda Editors Choice Prize)

*Call Me by Your Name* by André Aciman

## Humor *(from acid satire to funny ha-ha)*

*Divine Secrets of the Ya-Ya Sisterhood* by Rebecca Wells

*The Wishbones* by Tom Perrotta

*The House of God* by Samuel Shem

## War Stories *(oh the horror ... from ancient to modern)*

*The Iliad* by Homer (epic poem)

*Maus* by Art Spiegelman (graphic novel, Pulitzer Prize)

*The Red Badge of Courage* by Stephen Crane

*All Quiet on the Western Front* by Erich Maria Remarque

*Mister Roberts* by Thomas Heggen

*Suite Française* by Irène Némirovsky

*MASH* by Richard Hooker

*The Sorrow of War* by Bao Ninh

## Mélange *(a little of this and a little of that)*

*Fear of Flying* by Erica Jong

*Breakfast at Tiffany's* by Truman Capote

*Lonesome Dove* by Larry McMurtry (Pulitzer Prize)
*Crank* by Ellen Hopkins
*The Lovely Bones* by Alice Sebold

## HISTORICAL FICTION

### Romance *(love and longing set in the past)*

*Green Mansions* by W.H. Hudson
*Katherine* by Anya Seton and Philippa Gregory
*Ashes in the Wind* by Kathleen E. Woodiwiss

### Detective Thriller *(mysteries solved in pre-tech times)*

*The Alienist* by Caleb Carr
Hawkenlye mysteries by Alys Clare
*The Meaning of Night* by Michael Cox

### Adventure *(adrenaline mixed with exotic times and places)*

*Master and Commander* by Patrick O'Brian
*Tales of the South Pacific* by James Michener (Pulitzer Prize)
*The Physician* by Noah Gordon

### Family Saga *(the generations interact and intertwine)*

*Fall on Your Knees* by Ann-Marie MacDonald
*Gone With the Wind* by Margaret Mitchell (Pulitzer Prize)
*Roots* by Alex Haley (Pulitzer Prize)

### Drama *(history, heroism, and courage collide)*

*Schindler's List* by Thomas Keneally
*Arrow of God* by Chinua Achebe
*Raintree County* by Ross Lockridge Jr.

### Multi-Volume Historical Sagas *(etcetera etcetera)*

The Raj Quartet (*The Jewel in the Crown, The Day of the Scorpion, The Towers of Silence, A Division of Spoils*) by Paul Scott
*The Winds of War* and *War and Remembrance* by Herman Wouk
The Wales Trilogy (*Here Be Dragons, Falls the Shadow, The Reckoning*) by Sharon Kay Penman

## ROMANCE

### Creatures of the Night *(love, bloody love)*

*Dark Possession* by Christine Feehan

*Dark Lover* by J.R. Ward

*Jacob* by Jacquelyn Frank

## Historical Romance *(romance coupled with history)*

*Fires of Winter* by Johanna Lindsey

*The Talisman Ring* by Georgette Heyer

*The Rules of Seduction* by Madeline Hunter

## Regency Romance *(love and intrigue in early nineteenth-century England)*

*Night Secrets* by Kat Martin

*Regency Buck* by Georgette Heyer

*The Obedient Bride* by Mary Balogh

## Paranormal Romance *(making woo-woo)*

*A Wish in Time* by Laurel Bradley

*The Dream Thief* by Shana Abé

*A Love Out of Time* by Rick Adkins

## LGBT Romance *(boys together, girls together)*

*Lessons* by Kim Pritekel

*Turning Point* by Lara Zielinsky

*Strings Attached* by Nick Nolan

## Inspirational Romance *(chaste women chasing)*

*Indigo Waters* by Lisa Samson

*Guilty of Love* by Pat Simmons

*Courting Trouble* by Deeanne Gist

## Contemporary Romance *(mix and match love in modern settings)*

*Knock Me Off My Feet* by Susan Donovan

*Houston, We Have a Problem* by Erin McCarthy

*Truly Madly Yours* by Rachel Gibson

# MYSTERIES AND THRILLERS

## Detectives *(mysteries solved by PIs and others, sometimes amateurs)*

*Hot Six* by Janet Evanovich

*Deadlock* by Sara Paretsky

## Cozy *(minimum violence, maximum intrigue, amateur sleuth)*

*The Mirror Crack'd From Side to Side* by Agatha Christie

*Dead Days of Summer* by Carolyn Hart
*The No. 1 Ladies' Detective Agency* by Alexander McCall Smith

## Christian *(religious mysteries, both in and out of the cloister)*

*Murder, Mayhem & a Fine Man* by Claudia Mair Burney
*The Root of All Evil* by Brandt Dodson
*Irish Gold* by Andrew M. Greeley

## Noir *(hard-boiled guys, hard-boiled prose; darker, meaner streets than the average PI novel)*

*I, the Jury* by Mickey Spillane
*Devil in a Blue Dress* by Walter Mosley (Anisfield Wolf and O. Henry Awards)
*The Maltese Falcon* by Dashiell Hammett
*The Big Sleep* by Raymond Chandler

## Forensic *(mysteries solved with science and technology)*

*The Angel of Death* by Alane Ferguson
*Post Mortem* by Patricia Cornwell (Edgar Award)
*Break No Bones* by Kathy Reichs

## Police Procedural *(inside details of how cops solve crimes)*

*The Onion Field* by Joseph Wambaugh
*Voices: A Thriller* by Arnaldur Indridason
*Gorky Park* by Martin Cruz Smith

## Courtroom/Legal *(lawyers, lots of lawyers)*

*Presumed Innocent* by Scott Turow
*The Rainmaker* by John Grisham
*Proof of Intent* by William J. Coughlin and Walter Sorrells

## LGBT Mystery *(gay love played out in the arms of mystery)*

*Rising Storm* by Jlee Meyer
*Honor Under Siege* by Radclyffe
*Second Season* by Ali Vali

## Historical *(mysteries solved the old-fashioned way)*

*Badger's Moon* by Peter Tremayne
*The Widow's Tale* by Margaret Frazer
*Dark Star* by Alan Furst

**Thriller** *(racing pulse is de rigueur)*

*The Godfather* by Mario Puzo

*Hard Rain* by Barry Eisler (movie)

*The Secret Servant* by Daniel Silva

**Ghost Story** *(from hauntings to interactions with spirits)*

*Rebecca* by Daphne du Maurier

*Shadowland* by Peter Straub

**Horror** *(terror on the page and on the screen)*

*The Shining* by Stephen King

*The Exorcist* by William Peter Blatty

**Spy** *(what's none of their business is their business)*

*Kim* by Rudyard Kipling

*The Spy Who Came in From the Cold* by John le Carré (Edgar and Gold Dagger Awards)

*Goldfinger* by Ian Fleming

## SCIENCE FICTION

**Soft Science Fiction** *(stories grounded in social sciences such as psychology, sociology, and anthropology)*

*Flowers for Algernon* by Daniel Keyes

*The Martian Chronicles* by Ray Bradbury

*The Time Traveler's Wife* by Audrey Niffenegger

**Apocalypse and Postapocalypse** *(what happens during or after devastation—nuclear or otherwise)*

*The Road* by Cormac McCarthy (Pulitzer Prize)

*On the Beach* by Nevil Shute

*A Canticle for Leibowitz* by Walter M. Miller Jr. (Hugo Award)

**Cyberpunk** *(alienated characters vs. a high-tech world, often involving computer implants of one sort or another inserted directly into the body)*

*Neuromancer* by William Gibson (Hugo and Nebula Awards)

*Dune* by Frank Herbert (Hugo and Nebula Awards)

*Do Androids Dream of Electric Sheep?* by Philip K. Dick

**Feminist Science Fiction** *(gender roles explored in utopias and dystopias)*

*The Handmaid's Tale* by Margaret Atwood (Arthur C. Clarke Award)

*The Gate to Women's Country* by Sheri S. Tepper

*The Left Hand of Darkness* by Ursula K. Le Guin

## Comic Science Fiction *(skewed worlds filled with humor, both broad and subtle)*

*The Hitchhiker's Guide to the Galaxy* by Douglas Adams

*The Stainless Steel Rat* by Harry Harrison

*Good Omens* by Neil Gaiman and Terry Pratchett

## First Contact *(first encounters between humans and aliens)*

*Stranger in a Strange Land* by Robert A. Heinlein (Hugo Award)

*The Mote in God's Eye* by Larry Niven and Jerry Pournelle (Nebula and Hugo Awards)

*The Sparrow* by Mary Doria Russell (Arthur C. Clarke Award, James Tiptree Jr. Award, British Science Fiction Association Award)

## Colonization *(the creation of habitats beyond planet Earth and what happens when these colonies are formed or destroyed)*

The Mars Trilogy (*Red Mars, Green Mars, Blue Mars*) by Kim Stanley Robinson (British Science Fiction Association Award, Nebula and Hugo Awards)

*Moving Mars* by Greg Bear (Nebula Award)

*The Dragonriders of Pern* by Anne McCaffrey with Todd McCaffrey

## Military Science Fiction *(wars and combat, interstellar or otherwise)*

*The War of the Worlds* by H.G. Wells

*Old Man's War* by John Scalzi

*Forever Peace* by Joe Haldeman (Nebula and Hugo Awards)

## Time Travel *(travel into both past and future)*

*The Time Machine* by H.G. Wells

*Outlander* by Diana Gabaldon

*Slaughterhouse-Five* by Kurt Vonnegut

## Steampunk *(technology and rebellion, powered by steam)*

*The Golden Compass* by Philip Pullman

*The Diamond Age* by Neal Stephenson

*The League of Extraordinary Gentlemen* by Alan Moore and Kevin O'Neill (graphic novel)

**Hard Science Fiction** *(stories grounded in physics, astro-physics, and chemistry)*

*Contact* by Carl Sagan

*2001: A Space Odyssey* by Arthur C. Clarke

*Foundation* by Isaac Asimov

## FANTASY

*The Odyssey* by Homer

*Beowulf*

*The Divine Comedy* by Dante Alighieri

*The Once and Future King* by T.H. White

*The Lord of the Rings* by J.R.R. Tolkien

*The Chronicles of Narnia* by C.S. Lewis

*His Dark Materials* by Philip Pullman

*The Colour of Magic* by Terry Pratchett

*The Magic of Xanth* by Piers Anthony

*Everlost* by Neal Shusterman

*The Chronicles of Thomas Covenant* by Stephen R. Donaldson

Harry Potter series by J.K. Rowling

*Chrono Crusade* by Daisuke Moriyama (manga)

*Bleach* by Tite Kubo (manga)

## AUTOBIOGRAPHY AND MEMOIR

**Boot Strap** *(I once was down, but now I'm up)*

*The Pursuit of Happyness* by Chris Gardner, with contributions from Quincy Trope

*Rocket Boys* by Homer Hickam

*Born on the Fourth of July* by Ron Kovic

**Political** *(illuminations and explorations of interesting people and challenging times)*

*Dreams From My Father* by Barack Obama

*Mankiller: A Chief and Her People* by Wilma Mankiller with Michael Wallis

*The Haldeman Diaries: Inside the Nixon White House* by H.R. Haldeman

**Family** *(usually dysfunctional, since happy families are all alike)*

*Running With Scissors* by Augusten Burroughs

*The Glass Castle* by Jeannette Walls

*Brother, I'm Dying* by Edwidge Danticat

### Celebrity *(earned fame; we'll skip the other kind)*

*Born Standing Up: A Comic's Life* by Steve Martin

*Memories, Dreams, Reflections* by C.G. Jung with Aniela Jaffé

*Shock Value: A Tasteful Book About Bad Taste* by John Waters

### Travel *(running away from life or toward adventure in exotic places)*

*Tales of a Female Nomad: Living at Large in the World* by Rita Golden Gelman

*States of Mind* by Brad Herzog

*Seven Pillars of Wisdom* by T.E. Lawrence

### Survival *(the awesome power of human will)*

*Night* by Elie Wiesel (Nobel Laureate)

*Adrift: Seventy-Six Days Lost at Sea* by Steven Callahan

*The Pianist* by Władysław Szpilman

### Extraordinary Lives *(far above the madding crowd)*

*Tuesdays With Morrie* by Mitch Albom

*The Diary of a Young Girl* by Anne Frank

*My Land and My People: The Original Autobiography of His Holiness the Dalai Lama of Tibet* by the Dalai Lama

### Confession and Conversion *(pleas and apologias)*

*Blind Ambition* by John Dean

*Smashed: Story of a Drunken Girlhood* by Koren Zailckas

*In Retrospect* by Robert S. McNamara

### Spiritual Memoir *(peace at last)*

*The Seven Storey Mountain* by Thomas Merton

*The Cloister Walk* by Kathleen Norris

*Memoirs of a Spiritual Outsider* by Suzanne Clores

### Writer's Memoirs *(the yearning to speak and breathe free)*

*Speak, Memory* by Vladimir Nabokov

*Angela's Ashes* by Frank McCourt

*Manchild in the Promised Land* by Claude Brown

*Pilgrim at Tinker Creek* by Annie Dillard

## NEW JOURNALISM

*In Cold Blood* by Truman Capote (Edgar Award)
*The Armies of the Night* by Norman Mailer (Pulitzer Prize)
*The White Album* by Joan Didion
*Paper Lion* by George Plimpton
*The Electric Kool-Aid Acid Test* by Tom Wolfe
*Fear and Loathing in Las Vegas* by Hunter S. Thompson

## LITERARY FICTION

*Jane Eyre* by Charlotte Brontë
*Pride and Prejudice* by Jane Austen
*The Age of Innocence* by Edith Wharton (Pulitzer Prize)
*The Great Gatsby* by F. Scott Fitzgerald
*The Sun Also Rises* by Ernest Hemingway (Nobel Laureate)
*Look Homeward, Angel* by Thomas Wolfe
The Alexandria Quartet (*Justine, Balthazar, Mountolive,* and *Clea*) by Lawrence Durrell
*As I Lay Dying* by William Faulkner (Nobel Laureate)
*Ragtime* by E.L. Doctorow (NBCC Award)
*Atonement* by Ian McEwan (NBCC Award)
*The Last of the Just (Le Dernier des justes)* by André Schwarz–Bart
*The French Lieutenant's Woman* by John Fowles
*St. Urbain's Horseman* by Mordecai Richler
*The Catcher in the Rye* by J.D. Salinger
The Deptford Trilogy (*Fifth Business, The Manticore,* and *World of Wonders*) by Robertson Davies
*To Kill a Mockingbird* by Harper Lee (Pulitzer Prize)
*Sophie's Choice* by William Styron (Pulitzer Prize)
*The Golden Notebook* by Doris Lessing (Nobel Laureate)
*Catch-22* by Joseph Heller
*One Hundred Years of Solitude* by Gabriel García Márquez (Nobel Laureate)
*Plainsong* by Kent Haruf
*The Last Novel* by David Markson

# INDEX